THE
ENTREPRENEUR'S
SURVIVAL GUIDE

ROB STAM

ROB STAM

Copyright © 2017 by Rob Stam

This is a work of creative nonfiction. Any resemblance to actual persons, organizations, or events are purely coincidental.

All rights reserved by the author, including the right of reproduction in whole or in part in any form.

Cover design by Alex Tillard

ISBN 978-1544694634

Table of Contents

Introduction: The Great Adventure	5
Survival Key #1: Prepare Yourself	19
Survival key #2: Become a Master of Goal Setting	31
Survival Key #3: Get Your Team in Place	41
Survival Key #4: Know the Terrain	57
Survival Key #5: Prove Your Concept	73
Survival Key #6: Do the Math	87
Survival Key #7: Create Movement	101
Survival Key #8: Be Prepared for Challenges	121
Survival Key #9: Always Be Brand Conscious	139
Survival Key #10: Broaden Your Perspective	151
Acknowledgments	164

INTRODUCTION:

The Great Adventure

It was the summer of my 17th birthday. My father, in his 40s at the time, came up with the idea that he and I should do a thousand-mile bike trip from our home in Holland, Michigan to the Atlantic Ocean. The trip began by touching our wheels in Lake Michigan and took us across Michigan, through the southern tip of Ontario, Canada, and then across the states of New York, Vermont, and New Hampshire. The trip ended by touching our wheels in the water again, this time at Hampton Beach, NH. It was a stunningly beautiful way to see that section of America.

Perhaps the whole idea was part of some mid-life crisis to which I was not privy at the time; or perhaps it was a stroke of parenting genius that my father knew would create a series of memories and lessons that his son would look back upon countless times throughout his life. Regardless of the motive, we bought the padded shorts and bike helmets, and saddled up.

At 17, we are all immortal in our own minds. To me, this adventure would be as simple as jumping on a bike and pedaling like I'd done thousands of times before. A few years prior to this, my father and I had done a shorter trip of approximately 250 miles, so this seemed like no big deal. I did not participate much in the preparation, which included highlighting maps and guide books so we could plan our stops. This was ten years before GPS, and "Googling" had not been conceived of yet. Furthermore, a trip of this magnitude meant getting in shape, something I felt no need to do at the immortal age of 17.

It's easy to see how a thousand-mile, ten-day, father-and-son bike trip has the potential to serve as a metaphor for one's life, and as it pertains to the subject of this book, a metaphor for one's business endeavors. The ups and downs of mountains, turns in the road, unexpected encounters, flat tires, exhaustion, pain, weather, and more all create a canvas on which to paint the entrepreneurial adventure. So while the metaphor is somewhat obvious, it is only in retrospect that I can fully appreciate just how accurate a metaphor it is. This first monumental adventure of my life was frighteningly prophetic in how my journey as an entrepreneur would play out only a few years later.

Introduction

The stories from the bike trip are countless—too many to recap—but there is one particular moment that I can still visualize and even feel. Halfway through the state of New York, my dad had stopped to let me catch up (remember who failed to get in shape), and he was reviewing our map. I had my head down, pedaling as fast as I could, and I plowed right into him at 20+ miles an hour. As we sat in a pool of blood and mangled bike wheels we thought we were done for, until a good samaritan scooped us up. She brought us to the bike shop for bike repair and to the hospital for dad repair. Any normal person would have called it quits—I certainly wanted to—but my dad refused to give up.

We proceeded to finish the remaining 500 miles, me exhausted and him with a broken hand in a cast. Since that day he has also walked away from three plane crashes, so I'd dare say that *he* might actually be the immortal one.

> **If it's worth doing, it's worth doing despite the circumstances, no matter how difficult they seem.**

My dad is a survivor, and in that moment he gave me one of the most important lessons of my life: keep going. If it's worth doing, it's worth doing despite the circumstances, no matter how difficult they seem at that time.

Every adventure comes with lessons; you don't need a crash to learn something. But that's not the point of the adventure. The point is for it to be exactly what it's called: an adventure. Whether it be a bike trip, jumping out of an airplane, SCUBA diving, kayaking, mountain climbing, or whatever else, the reason for the adventure is that you crave it and you won't be satisfied unless you do it. You don't need to rationalize it, you simply have to do it. In fact, you can't fully rationalize it. The only rationale for adventure is the reality that the result is unknown. As one definition of the word states, adventure is to take a chance. Had we known we would crash halfway through we might have said no to that bike trip and missed out on one of the greatest adventures of our lives.

Entrepreneurship is also an adventure and, interestingly enough, is defined by that same concept of taking a chance. In fact, no good definition of the word entrepreneur exists without the word *risk* (a point I'll elaborate on later in this book). For entrepreneurs, our careers must be an adventure, full of risk and comparatively void of the predictable. Money does not satisfy, and accolades are fleeting. We crave the adventure of getting out of the predicable box in which most of us in America are raised: go to school, get good grades, get into a good college, get a job, save money, etc.

Introduction

Despite the hint of cynicism in that last sentence, there is absolutely nothing wrong with that "normal" way of life, unless you're wired to be an entrepreneur. The thought of normal, safe, and what some people would consider wise, makes us nauseous. At our very core we are wired to observe what the masses do, and then do the opposite. On the flip side of that, the thought of risking everything with no certainty will leave others up at night in cold sweats. No one should ever claim that one way is better than the other—all we can do is be true to which side we belong on and realize that we are equally dependent on each other.

The problem, however, is that while many of us entrepreneurs are willing to be adventuresome and take a chance, we are reckless in doing so. Any seasoned adventurer will tell you that recklessness will eventually catch up to you. Reckless people don't last long as mountain climbers, SCUBA divers, bikers, and kayakers, and they don't last long as entrepreneurs either. The key to taking risks in any adventure is knowing how to survive and keep going. If you're going to take risks, you do it because it is the very risk that drives you. But if you are wise, those risks are calculated, and you are prepared to deal with them when they impact you.

Part of the reason I think many entrepreneurs are reckless in risk-taking is because the "system" doesn't cater to risk takers for obvious reasons: they represent the minority of the population. (I don't mean to sound derogatory with the word *system*, ours the world's finest by a long shot, but I'm not sure what else to call it.) Our schools and colleges exist to prepare us for the career world. And while much of that education is essential in entrepreneurship, you really need to step outside of that system at some point to really learn. For that small percentage of Americans who choose to do so, there is very little support that exists other than just "taking a chance." Those who are good at it, for the most part, are doing it and not teaching it.

Ironically, however, that very same system is entirely dependent upon the entrepreneur succeeding. We need our entrepreneurs to build successful businesses that create jobs, and we demand a lot from those businesses. It's the responsibility of the business owner to provide a good working environment with stability and benefits. Those who succeed end up paying the highest tax rates in our society as well. And that's all fine and good because the system also allows for great financial benefits for those who do succeed. Even so, the fact is, those financial benefits will never justify the emotional risks. You are an entrepreneur because you have to do it or you'll regret it for the rest of your life. That should be the only motivation you need to be more prepared.

I have been a certified SCUBA instructor for most of my adult life and on a regular basis I find myself engaging in the topic of diving. "I've always wanted to try SCUBA diving," is the most common thing I hear. Most who utter that phrase have the same fears. And, truth be told, those fears are justified. There is a lot that can go wrong. Exposing your body to two to four times the normal pressure while breathing compressed air in an environment where you are no longer the top of the food chain has some obvious hazards. But what many people don't realize is how unlikely it is that you will be hurt when SCUBA diving. Why? Because 90% of all SCUBA training is based around survival. The books, videos, pool training, and open water training are not designed to make you a great diver, they are designed to keep you alive. And it works; statistically it is one of the safest hobbies you can take up. SCUBA diving is an amazing experience—the most untouched part of our world is underwater. But if you don't learn the keys to surviving first you'll never get to experience it.

As it is in the water, so it is in business. The more advanced you want to be as a diver, the more risks you need to prepare for. The more successful you want to be in business, the more risks you need to prepare for.

> *The more successful you want to be in business, the more risks you need to prepare for.*

My hope then with this book is to play a small role in correcting that preparedness problem for you, wherever you are in your entrepreneurship journey. While no single book or author can prepare you for the specific risks at every level of business, I'm hoping some of my personal experiences as a survivor—and the lessons I've learned as a result—can help you in your journey.

Before I go into my survival story, it should be noted that survival is not the point of business. The only reason I frame the conversation around survival is because if you don't figure that part out first, you'll never get what you really want as an entrepreneur—a successful business.

Most entrepreneurs fail (Studies show that 80% of businesses don't survive five years, and over 90% don't last ten years). There are many reasons for that, but I'd argue that the single greatest reason for the high failure rate is that most of them only fail once, instead of failing as many times as it takes. The opposite of success is not failure, it's quitting. The crash on our bike trip was a failure for a matter of hours, but for over 20 years it's been part of a thousand-mile success story.

My first crack at entrepreneurship came in 2002. I was an employee of a company that was struggling financially. A fellow employee and I thought we could turn it around, so we took the helm. Over a period of 18 months, a myriad of scenarios played out related to banking, vendors, and taxes, which led to the company being shut down. Clients were left hanging, and over 30 employees were laid off. The result of this experience for me was a year-long lawsuit of over half a million dollars and an IRS lien that crippled my life for over 10 years. I can unpack this experience into a series of bad decisions and mistakes, but ultimately there is a single common factor that led to this collapse: my partner and I suffered from reckless optimism. We did not have the experience and knowledge to run a business. We had vision, we had charisma, and we had ideas. But we were not ready for entrepreneurship.

Still, we survived. Wounded, but still optimistic, I continued in business with my partner. We dabbled in a few ventures, primarily in the music industry, in which we both had a background. We jumped on the real estate bandwagon with everyone else as a means to fund our ambitions. It was 2005 at this time, and everyone was buying houses. TV shows were created about flipping houses. Remember those years? And then 2007 happened. Housing values plummeted, and like millions of other people, we were destroyed. My name was on title for multiple homes, all now devalued at least 30% below their mortgaged amounts with tenants who'd lost their incomes and couldn't pay rent. Construction projects were halted, subcontractors filed lawsuits against me, banks foreclosed, and the rest is history.

My family and I were living in a beautiful custom home at that time, which we had built a few years prior. Our son was just three years old. The past due bills and shut-off notices were coming in the mail daily. My wife didn't want to open them, but one day while I was out of town she finally did. As she opened the mail she realized that the gas was going to be shut off in a matter of days and the electricity wasn't far behind. She called her father in tears who graciously gave her his credit card information to pay them. In addition to the shut-off notices, I had a total of 17 lawsuits filed against me in a matter of approximately 30 days. We were on a first-name basis with the process server.

Earlier that year we were planning to upgrade from that custom home. We were renovating a six-thousand-square-foot home on five acres of lakefront property. I was driving an S-Class Mercedes. We had a 34-foot boat in a marina and took expensive vacations. But, by October of 2007 we had filed bankruptcy, and we lost it all: the houses, cars, business, lifestyle, security, income. It was all gone.

Like my bike crash, before my entrepreneurial crash I thought I was immortal. I was pedaling with my head down, paying no attention to the dangers ahead. I was reckless and unprepared, and it nearly cost me everything

I had. Of course there were other factors, such as highly unethical banking practices that destroyed an entire market, and business colleagues who left me hanging. I can point fingers all day long, but ultimately it comes back to that one simple concept: preparedness, or more accurately, a lack of it.

There was a theme playing out in my life. It wasn't that I lacked the talent or skill, I lacked the discipline to prepare. Lack of preparation can literally kill you in any adventure, and it can metaphorically kill you in entrepreneurship, as was the case in my life.

In six short years I experienced an exciting rise to entrepreneurship, and then a dramatic fall. Despite the failures, there were successes in between that made me some money. I don't talk much about those because, ironically, they possess very little educational value. It's the failures that taught me how to be good at entrepreneurship, not the successes. Those six years provided a greater education than any college could offer (at least that's what people with lots of letters behind their names tell me). What I learned about organizational structures, budgets, venture capital, banking, tax laws, leadership, human resources, book-keeping, and a thousand other topics was worth the "tuition" I paid. That period of my life hurt beyond words, and it's traumatic and embarrassing to think about. But I learned.

Then there were those lessons about life that transcend the business lessons. One of them was this: life is too short to be lived as someone else. If you only get one thing from this entire book, I hope it's that. On multiple occasions it was very tempting to give up and turn my back on being an entrepreneur. But that would mean turning my back on me.

One of my favorite songs of all time is *The Boxer* by Paul Simon. The last verse goes like this:

> *In the clearing stands a boxer*
> *And a fighter by his trade*
> *And he carries the reminders*
> *Of ev'ry glove that laid him down*
> *And cut him till he cried out*
> *In his anger and his shame*
> *"I am leaving, I am leaving"*
> *But the fighter still remains.*

Like the boxer, I have felt beat up. But lest I blame someone else for *ev'ry glove that cut me til I cried out* it was me who chose to step in the ring. And once you choose do the same, you have to possess the same commitment as the boxer. You have to become a fighter and, whenever you feel like leaving, remember, the fighter still remains.

I don't mean to over-dramatize the role of the entrepreneur. But I will say there have been several times in my career when I felt this way, just as Paul Simon did as a singer when he wrote it. I know dozens of other business owners who would say the same thing.

Chances are you'll never experience what I did and have an epic crash. Perhaps you've had some false starts in your entrepreneurial journey, which can actually be worse than a crash. When the failure is more subtle, it's easier to view it as a series of mistakes or circumstances beyond your control instead of an experience that you need to learn from. You may even look at yourself as a victim instead of as the culprit. And, you may just give up. But I hope you don't.

If you're truly wired to be an entrepreneur and you turn your back on your entrepreneurial ambitions, at some point the feeling of failure will catch up to you. It may be later in life when the words, "I wish I would have…" come out of your mouth. You'd give anything to go back 20 years and try again. Instead of a crash, you'll experience a crisis. A crisis of identity because you lost sight of who you truly are. You opted for stability when you needed adventure.

To be an entrepreneur, you must first embrace the fact that you are an adventurer: you are a risk taker, which automatically puts you in the minority of people. Then, you must know how to survive, to fully understand the risks and to be prepared for them. But whether you succeed or fail (never quit!), it's worth it to go to sleep every night knowing you lived the adventure and gave it your all.

Success in business only happens when passion, preparedness, and opportunity intersect. The rest of this book is written in the form of ten Survival Keys to help you align those three things. As you read, I encourage you to replace my examples with your own. Take notes and use this book as it's truly meant to be: a guide that will help you plan ahead, avoid common mistakes, and develop you into the entrepreneur that you know you can be.

SURVIVAL KEY #1

Prepare Yourself

In 2008 I was sitting in a favorite local pub with my long-time friend and mentor, Greg. We hadn't spoken much in the previous few years, but our paths had merged again and he was stepping in to help me figure out how to pick up the pieces following my epic entrepreneurial crash. As we were discussing business and career plans, I became lost in the moment, and my mind began to wander as I processed his advice. So much so, in fact, that I failed to notice his palm rise and slam against the particle board wall of the booth. The staccato smack brought me back from wherever I had wandered off to, and the pub seemed to grow silent as I waited for his next words.

"Rob," he said, "You need to build something!" He pointed back to the wall. "This is just a booth wall in a restaurant, but someone can look at it and say, 'I built this.'

Rob, what have you built?" The question pierced through my craft-beer-enhanced state and firmly grasped my attention. Those words have surfaced in my mind countless times since then. In fact, that conversation eventually led to me writing my first book as I pondered not just my own destiny, but that of my entire generation—raised in affluence, now taking our turn at leadership following the great recession.

As I listened to Greg's words, with recent memories of bankruptcy filling my mind, I could not have predicted the future trajectory of my career. I certainly could not have guessed that I would go on to create a company that would help others succeed in business—let alone write a book about it. I only knew in that moment, under the bar lights, that my heart seemed to come alive at his words. *What have you built?*

Here's why this question is so important when talking about entrepreneurship: successful entrepreneurs have something to show for their efforts. You can't go on calling yourself an entrepreneur forever if all you have is ideas and dreams. Eventually something has to turn into a tangible product or service. Where is the evidence that you're an entrepreneur? Can you call yourself a mountain climber if all you do is go to the climbing gym? No. You're someone who dreams of climbing a mountain, or perhaps just someone who likes to tell people you're a climber. But will you ever actually be a real climber?

To be an entrepreneur, you need to get past the idea phase and start figuring out the difference between an idea and a business. Years ago I heard the phrase, "Ideas are like armpits; everyone has two of them and most of them stink." Encouraging, isn't it? That statement may be a little harsh, but it contains an element of truth—perhaps more than we care to admit. I have seen a hundred bad ideas for every single good one. People with ideas are dreamers, people with businesses are entrepreneurs.

I've met a lot of people who like the idea of *being* an entrepreneur, but I'm not sure they really like the idea of *becoming* one. There's a difference between being and becoming. Why? Owning a business is different than building one. It's similar to those who say they want to lose weight but never do. They don't want to actually lose the weight, or they'd be doing it; they just want to be thinner. The "being" is easy. The "becoming" is hard.

So are you interested in *being* or *becoming*? Do you know? Becoming a true entrepreneur must begin with honest self analysis. There is no greater asset to the entrepreneur than self awareness. When you're self aware you can handle both the successes and challenges in business. In 2008, I had to discover the common themes and behaviors that had determined the trajectory of my life to that point, and would therefore determine the trajectory of my future endeavors. In my journey, I had to hit reset and change my status from a failed entrepreneur to a successful one. Before you go any further in business, you need to first figure out if you're really ready to do this, or, if you just like the idea of doing it. If your history doesn't lay a course for a successful future, like mine didn't, then guess what? You need to change something about yourself first.

There's a question I suggest you ask yourself to start the "becoming" process: Does entrepreneurship appeal to you for the right reasons? Why are you doing this? What is it about you that craves being an entrepreneur? If it's not because you honestly think you can and should build something that the market will support, then check your motives before taking any risk. A great idea won't propel you—you have to propel the idea.

> *A great idea won't propel you, you have to propel the idea.*

Many of us want to be entrepreneurs to prove something to someone else. We often expend far too much energy thinking that we can reconcile something in our past with our future. Perhaps you dropped out of college and you believe that by starting a business you can prove everyone wrong who doubted your decision. I tried that one. Or perhaps you got fired and you want to show your former boss that you can start your own business and do it better than he could. In fact, you'll put him out of business within five years! I've heard that one at least a dozen times as well.

If you can relate to those motivations, then you will have to become very good at leaving the baggage of your past where it belongs and only taking the knowledge and wisdom you've gained from it forward. By baggage, I'm specifically referring to feelings of regret, animosity, and resentment. Those feelings do you no good. In fact they do just the opposite. They will skew your decision making to be emotion-driven instead of logic-driven.

The real reason Greg had that talk with me back in 2008 wasn't because he was trying to show me how I had nothing to show for my entrepreneurial ambitions. He was showing me that the reason I had nothing to show for them was because I had been doing it for all the wrong reasons. My motives were misaligned. I wasn't interested in entrepreneurship because I believed in building a business. I really just wanted the adventure and accolades associated with it.

At that time in my life I had a tendency to crave the approval of others at an unhealthy level. I wanted people to like me and would compromise good practice for that acceptance. I would take foolish risks and avoid tough decisions in the pursuit of acceptance. I wanted to be one of the cool kids with the nice toys that everyone wanted to be around. I wasn't focused on building, but instead was focused on how I could impress people. The more I earned and spent, the more accepted I felt I would be and the more conflict I could avoid. But a life built on the approval of others will, ironically, end up being very lonely and unfulfilled.

Greg was calling me out for being a fake entrepreneur. To change that, I had to change me. I had to realize how to drop the past and rediscover a better version of myself before I could ever succeed in business. In this process, I identified three specific areas in my life that I had to change in order to get on the path to becoming a real entrepreneur.

1. I had to change my surroundings.

Two of the most important words you will ever learn in business are *right people* (a point I'll revisit multiple times in this book). In my past, I surrounded myself with people who did not complement my skill set or personality. I'm not suggesting they were, or are, bad people. In fact many of them are still friends and are doing quite well in business. But I found myself simply along for a ride and a bit out of control. I was making foolish decisions and putting myself in situations in which my skill sets were not maximized, and my character was being compromised.

If I was to ever figure out who I really was and what I could really accomplish, I had to regain control of my existence. I made the decision to walk away from every business venture or idea I was a part of and go out on my own to do some soul searching. I parted ways with my former business partner and our various colleagues, and completely changed my surroundings.

2. I had to get very honest about my strengths and weaknesses.

I found myself asking some very difficult and honest questions. First of all, what was I good at? The truth is that most of us are only really good at a few things. Figuring that out is essential because only then can you surround yourself with the right people who will complement those skills and vice versa. Separating myself from certain people and circumstances allowed me to regain a healthy perspective on my own skills and weaknesses.

I have found that I excel at setting the vision for a business. From there, I can strategize what steps are necessary to make that vision a reality, and I can lead a team in the proper direction. But I have many shortcomings. For example, I am not a manager. The thought of assigning and tracking a hundred tasks for ten people puts me in a cold sweat. If I was going to succeed, I had to come to terms with that as a weakness and had to develop strategies—in this case, hiring people proficient in management—to compensate.

A more painful way of digging deeper into identifying your strengths is to ask yourself this question: Am I necessary? The truth was that, from an economic standpoint, I really wasn't necessary in 2008. I wanted to be, but I wasn't. I'm not implying that I wasn't necessary as person, but in the world of business I wasn't adding value to anyone. At best, I was a master manipulator. I could sell and I could leverage. Cash, real estate, opportunities, and relationships were there for my gain. I didn't actually offer any service or product of value. This needed to change if I was going to pilot the ship of a new venture. At the heart of the entrepreneur is someone who adds value, otherwise there's no point in being one.

3. I had to redefine success.

Our paradigm of success becomes most healthy when we divorce business success from personal success. A business is an entity that makes money by delivering a valuable product or service. In turn, that business can make a positive impact on a community by providing jobs and supporting other businesses and causes. The ultimate measure of success for any business is one thing: profit. If you have that, your business can be called a success. However, just because someone runs a successful business does not make him or her a successful person. Business does not exist to validate people and make them successful; it exists to make money.

Personal success cannot be dependent on that, or it will lead to poor, emotion-driven decisions on the part of the business owner. The organization and you are two separate characters in the same story. Personal success can be measured by a number of metrics that are different for each individual. Personal success is an attitude and not a destination. You don't arrive at success due to some financial number. You can't obtain it, you can only choose it. All too often we allow others to define success for us by making income or notoriety synonymous with success.

Ultimately, personal success comes down to living your life as the person you truly are and not what anyone else tells you that you should be. In 2016 I took a solo trip to one of my favorite places on earth, Moab, Utah. In between the mountain biking, hiking, and paddling the Colorado River I took some time to write three lists. First were the things that I was truly passionate about—the things that are an authentic part of who I am. The second was a list of things that I spend most of my time doing. And the third was a list of things in my life that I just really don't like doing or being a part of.

As one would expect, I discovered that I spend most of my time doing things that I don't want to do. Not that they are bad things, they just don't truly bring me fulfillment or happiness. Some of them are necessary as part of life and business, and I'm not delusional that any of us can live our lives only doing things we love. But, what's the point of living if we let it get too far out of balance? As an entrepreneur, I encourage you to ask yourself this question on a regular basis: will you own the business or will the business own you? If it doesn't truly fulfill you, then it owns you.

Write down a set of metrics to measure your personal success. This may include family goals, hobbies, travel, charitable support, your health, your attitude, and any number of variables. Some of those may have to be delayed while you grow a business, and some may change and evolve, but you should live by them from day one. Start defining success by those and not by the profitability of a business or by your income. In fact, when writing your metrics, leave money and income out of it.

Money is just a tool. You can make as much as you want if you're willing to work hard enough and set yourself up for success. Also, no matter how much money you make, you'll always wish there was more. If you can't figure out how to be a successful person with $10,000 a year you'll never learn how to be one with $1,000,000 a year.

Those were my three big steps: 1. changing my surroundings, 2. getting very honest about my strengths and weaknesses and 3. redefining success. Yours may be different, or you may have none at all. But the point is to take time to become self-aware. The hardest part in making an honest assessment about yourself is that when you do, you'll also learn that it takes a tremendous amount of energy to change. If your past concerns you, the future might seem even scarier. That's the very reason why I am so transparent about my shortcomings: I want you to see that there is hope, no matter what. But it takes work.

Think about New Year's resolutions for a minute. Earlier I mentioned the difference between wanting to lose weight and wanting to be thinner. Most people fail at seeing their resolutions through to fruition for that reason. They don't appreciate how hard it is to make changes in their lives. They just get excited about the prospect of the result. This is why so many people look for a miracle pill to take the pounds off instead of sustained dieting and exercise. Being overweight is usually a symptom of behavior. I used to weigh 60 pounds more than I do now. Laziness and unhealthy eating habits had to be replaced by a better diet and increased physical activity.

Many entrepreneurs face a similar problem. It takes a tremendous commitment to change yourself and become a great entrepreneur; that's why there are so few of them. If you're honest about your shortcomings in any area of life, and you want something to change, then you will have to change at least one behavior. There's no pill that can do it for you, and it may be more difficult than you realize. So if you're about to venture into the world of business ownership for the first time, you may just need to admit that you don't know what you are doing yet. And if you're venturing in for a second or third time, I hope you've already realized you need to change something and are well on your way to doing so.

Perhaps that's why you're reading this book. Maybe you need to own up to your past failures like I did, or maybe you need to stop clinging to your past successes thinking they alone will propel you forward. You may have to learn how to leave all of that in the past. You may have to become incredibly self-aware about some behaviors, attitudes, or perspectives that you need to change. Now is the time to get honest with yourself and prepare to make the transition from dreamer to entrepreneur.

SURVIVAL KEY #2

Become a Master of Goal Setting

On May 25, 1961, President John F. Kennedy gave a famous speech to a joint session of Congress where he stated these transformative words: "I believe that this nation should commit itself to achieving the goal, before this decade is out, of landing a man on the moon and returning him safely to the earth." I'm not sure we can find a better example of a more clearly defined, obtainable, and well-articulated goal anywhere in human history than in the speeches President Kennedy gave leading up to the moon landing. I encourage you to take the time to search for some of them and read the transcripts. To fully appreciate the magnitude of the moment, one also needs to watch Walter Cronkite's on-air commentary in which he says: "For thousands of years now it's been man's dream to walk on the moon. Right now after seeing it happen, knowing it happened, it still seems like a dream."

So what changed walking on the moon from a dream into a reality? What allowed humankind to embark on this, the greatest of all adventures? Certainly there were many factors related to technological innovation, foreign competition, and advances in our understanding of space. But I believe the catalyst—the single greatest factor that turned it from a dream to reality—was the logical, believable, and clearly articulated goal by President Kennedy. All the knowledge and experience in the world is only as good as the goals that surround it. Clear goals are what move ideas out of our dreams and into our reality. And I believe the same can be true for you and your dreams as an entrepreneur.

> *All the knowledge and experience in the world is only as good as the goals that surround it.*

Many entrepreneurs, especially in their first go-around, don't fully understand what they are trying to accomplish. They have ambitions, such as: "We're going to get this product into retail stores across the country." But that's no more obtainable than if JFK had just said, "I want us to put someone on the moon." Sure, people would have been excited about the possibility, and his charisma may have gotten some buy-in for a while, but if that's as far as it went, we'd still be dreaming about the moon instead of planning for Mars.

Some of Kennedy's speeches discussed how going to the moon played into in the greater narrative of "freedom vs. tyranny." He had specific action items, including budget resources, the teams of people he would need, and specific commitments the American people would have to make. Furthermore, he outlined benefits such as business growth and job creation that inspired stronger commitment to the goal. This was more than ambitious hype; it was thought-out in both purpose and process and supported by smaller actionable items and benefits that the American people could commit to. There was a team of intelligent people supporting it who knew what their specific roles would be. Then, in the hands of an influential leader, it came to life.

One of the reasons many dreams never make it to reality is that we frequently fail to understand the difference between an ambition and a goal. This is a common sticking point for aspiring entrepreneurs. We get too caught up in the ambition—the dream—and fail to create actual, attainable goals. Having a business in five years that produces a million dollars in sales annually to 100 customers at a 25% margin is a little closer to a goal, but even that is still in the ambition stage. From there you still need to work backwards and define the actionable steps it will take to achieve it.

Another way to think about ambitions is that they are the potential positive side effects of reaching goals. Profit is the ultimate definition of a successful business and your ultimate goal, but that's too lofty to really be a goal. Wealth and influence are not goals, they are results. Changing that perspective helps you see that a lot of what you thought were goals in your mind were actually ambitions, whether in the form of dreams or the benefits of reaching your goals.

So how do you make the leap from ambitions to creating attainable goals?

There are multiple resources and strategies on how to set goals effectively. Countless books have been written on the topic, and you can find any number of blogs you can reference to help you become more structured with your goal setting. You may be familiar with the commonly taught S.M.A.R.T. Methodology, which stands for Specific, Measurable, Assignable, Realistic, and Time-Related. (I've also seen people substitute in Attainable and Relevant). That methodology has proven to be a great place to start for many in the business world.

Your ambition may be to take a product to the national retail market, and it may be possible, but is it *Realistic* in the foreseeable future, or within your desired *Time Frame*? Do you have control over that ambition, and can you build smaller, *Assignable* steps within it? Or, are you hoping for a third party who will make it happen for you like a singer who hopes for a record deal? Get *Specific* about what channels you will take to get to that market, how you will enter those channels, and who *Specifically* will be *Assigned* to lead that effort. Once you've done that, you need to *Measure* your progress.

Another very important part of goal setting is to not confuse personal goals and success with business goals and success. In the previous chapter we discussed the definition of personal success. Your personal goals should be based on your values and desires for your time on this earth and what you'd like to leave for the generations that follow. Business goals, on the other hand, should be defined by what *the marketplace* wants. I believe a primary reason for overly vague business goals is that many entrepreneurs build their goals around their personal ambitions instead of the opportunities in the market.

Let's look at an example: A homebuilder can have a goal of building fifty houses a year because he loves building houses. He can equip himself with the necessary tools and a team of subcontractors, but if the community he lives in doesn't support that many homes, and he's one of ten other builders competing for the business, his goal is misguided, and he will fail to reach it. He can go to every success seminar, read every business book, have a list of credentials a mile long, and write a business plan worthy of a Pulitzer, but if the market doesn't want fifty new houses a year, none of it matters. Your goals have to fit the market (or they need to be adjusted to work within the market), or you need to expand your market to achieve your goals.

Whether your potential marketplace is your own hometown or the entire globe, goal setting in business demands an in-depth understanding of the size and characteristics of that market. Survival Key #4 unpacks this thought further, but for the sake of setting goals, first understand that the hunches or gut feelings you have about your potential market are solely based on your perspective. Until you've done the research, that perspective is far too limited to build a business around.

Perspective is one of the most powerful forces in the human experience. In business, our ability to alter our own perspective and gain perspectives from others will make us far better equipped to succeed. Taking that a step further, changing your perspective with real data is what will keep you from making emotional and subjective decisions, and instead helps you make profitable decisions. Understanding the market potential for your business will demand facts that can only come from research and calculated effort, but it's an effort worthy of your time. If market research doesn't sound like your cup of tea, get help; but as the leader of your business, you have to understand your market and build your goals around it.

Still, for all the time you put into crafting SMART goals that are based on what the market wants, they are only as valuable as your willingness to commit to them.

In 1519 Hernán Cortés landed his ships on the shores of the Yucatan with approximately 600 men with the intention of claiming the land and its treasure for the Spanish Crown. As his conquest of the Aztec empire commenced across Mexico, some of his soldiers plotted mutiny and a retreat to Cuba in his ships. When Cortés received word of the plot, he captured the men and ordered all of his ships to be scuttled, removing any possibly of escape. When the remaining men asked how they would return home to Spain with the Aztec gold, he replied: "If we are going home, we're going home in their ships." Despite being vastly outnumbered and on foreign soil, Cortés committed to a goal and refused to leave room for any option other than success. Within two years they had begun the Spanish colonization of Mexico.

While western expansion at the expense of indigenous people creates an ugly chapter in human history that I don't want to edify with that example, please don't miss the forest for the trees. No goal is worth setting if you're not committed to it. As the owner of a business, you may well have to "scuttle your ships," whatever those ships may be.

I have worked with more entrepreneurs who fail to commit than who do commit. There are two different scenarios that seem to play out consistently with those who fail to commit: First is the *now is not the right time* scenario. Second is the *there's one more thing to do before we launch* scenario. The common theme in both cases is fear.

In the first scenario, there is typically an outside variable that interrupts the commitment. They are excited about the prospect of starting a business, and will even go through the work to formulate a plan and get the foundation laid. But then a financial situation, family dynamic, or some other factor suddenly puts it all on hold. There will always be reasons and excuses to keep you from moving forward. Plan on it. Successful entrepreneurs move forward in spite of those. Get your finances in order, make sure those close to you know and understand your commitment, don't let anything get in your way, and leave no room to blame anyone else if you don't stick it out.

The second scenario is a little more complicated to rationalize, but I can personally relate to it more than the first. Sometimes it's the fear of failure that holds us back, but in my experience it's actually the fear of success that paralyzes the entrepreneur. This could be called the *fail-*

ure to launch syndrome. What if this actually works? Am I ready to handle it? The actual work of running a business is scary, so we'd prefer to just keep innovating. There always seems to be an opportunity on the horizon that we have to pursue instead of just buckling down and putting our plan into action.

Entrepreneurs are visionaries by nature. One of the hardest things for us to do is to put blinders on for short periods of time so we can make progress. We must become self-disciplined enough to resist temptations, ignore distractions, and focus on progress. There will always be opportunities, but only those who are focused and committed to progress will be able to take advantage of them.

One of my favorite characters to emerge in the last several years is Jack Sparrow from *The Pirates of the Caribbean* movie series. In the first movie there is a great scene where he and Elizabeth Swan are stranded on an island drinking rum by the fire after being marooned there and left to die. Jack utters these words: "That's what a ship is you know, not a keel and a hold and a deck and sails…that's what a ship needs. But what a ship is, what the Black Pearl really is, is freedom."

Jack Sparrow is an interesting character. Despite all of his ridiculous flaws you cannot argue the fact that Jack always knows what he wants. He is extremely calculated in his behavior, always working an angle that comes back to one thing: The Black Pearl. He never stops moving towards that goal. But why? Is the Black Pearl his ultimate desire? Not at all. Freedom is his ultimate desire: the freedom of the sea that can only be achieved, for him, on the Black Pearl. Jack Sparrow's goal is clear, and he is unwavering in his quest to attain that goal. To him it is more than a goal, it is an essential part of who he is and he can't be happy until he has it.

For all the effort it takes to research and establish goals, the effort is only as valuable as your ability to combine specific goals with a strong commitment to achieving them. To transition from being a dreamer to entrepreneur, you need to create realistic, attainable goals, and commit to those goals with a passion. Be organized and detailed, but don't ever let the dream die.

Set goals like Jack Kennedy, commit to them like Cortés, and focus on them with the unwavering passion of Jack Sparrow.

SURVIVAL KEY #3
Get Your Team in Place

Jim Collins, best-selling author of the book, *Good to Great* presents this analogy for leading a business:

You are a bus driver. The bus, your company, is at a standstill, and it's your job to get it going. You have to decide where you're going, how you're going to get there, and who's going with you. Most people assume that great bus drivers (business leaders) immediately start the journey by announcing to the people on the bus where they're going—by setting a new direction or by articulating a fresh corporate vision. In fact, leaders of companies that go from good to great start not with "where" but with "who." They start by getting the right people on the bus, the wrong people off the bus, and the right people in the right seats. And they stick with that discipline—first the people, then the direction.

In the first chapter I mentioned that the two most important words in business are *right people*. I can't emphasize enough how true this is in every aspect of a project: employees, partners, clients, suppliers, bankers, attorneys, advisors, etc. If we are wise, we realize that we will always need the expertise and effort of others to succeed. No matter how small your business is at the moment, you need to fill the gaps in your knowledge, ability, or capacity in some area, and probably in multiple areas. One of the most common mistakes I see with entrepreneurs is that they fill those gaps with the wrong people. In some cases, that's easily fixed. If you find out six months from now that you've got the wrong banker, you can change that with minimal interruption. But if it's a business partner or employee, the subjects of this chapter, you have a greater challenge.

When talking about *right people*, the business partnership is probably the most important relationship to address and it will usually create the most anxiety with entrepreneurs at every level. I, along with many others, have made the mistake of choosing business partners because of availability, instead of capability. Entrepreneurs have a tendency to look at partners through the lens of shared optimism and personality type instead of usefulness. We're drawn to those who fuel our excitement when we should be drawn to those whom we can identify as being truly essential to the organization.

> **There is only one reason to have a business partner: because they solve a problem.**

There is only one reason to have a business partner: because they solve a problem. Many think that having someone to share the burden of starting a business *is* solving a problem. In most cases, that's simply not true. In fact, giving up a percentage of your business to make it easier on you actually makes you weaker instead of making the business stronger. We may feel more confident having someone at our side, but in reality we're compensating for insecurities instead of becoming stronger in the areas where we are weak.

My observation from watching hundreds of partnerships over the years, and having a few of my own, is that partnerships built around two or three people who primarily just share a passion or belief are the ones that struggle. It's the businesses where the partners have clearly defined expectations and complementing skill sets that tend to work.

If you are considering a partnership, I believe there are three problems you can use to evaluate your potential partner(s). If you can't find where they solve any of these, then you may need to rethink having that person as a partner:

1. **Financial.** Your business needs capital and he has it or can get it for you.

2. **Ability.** She possesses a unique skill set or level of experience beyond what you can reasonably hire in an employee in the time frame needed.

3. **Connections.** He holds the keys to a market that is essential to your success, and the only way to open that door is for him to have a stake in the company.

But even solving these three problems may not demand a partnership. I'm not suggesting you have to avoid partnership at any cost, but you do need to weigh the immediate value of it against the long-term return you're giving a partner. Almost any problem can be solved by hiring the right person or through some sort of third-party relationship. For example, a private equity partner who brings financial investment may sound appealing, but there are other ways to obtain capital. You have to truly evaluate the necessity of it against the value of that ownership you're giving up, instead of signing the deal because you feel like it immediately solves all your problems.

Business partnerships must always equate to a dollar value. If a partner is bringing more money to the table than you, you have to somehow quantify your contribution to the partnership so they don't feel like they are taking all the risk. If they are not bringing financial investment, you still have to look at what they are bringing from a perspective of financial worth. What is the value of the business today and what is a realistic forecast for it in the future? What are they contributing in relation to that? Ask yourself how valuable it is, not just how convenient it is.

Value is a difficult thing to determine, especially when you're a start-up business or a young company. There is no exact science, and there are many variables that can contribute to a valuation of an idea or young company such as: assets, time invested, uniqueness of ideas, experience in the industry or market, unique skills, or ability to borrow money. Following some of the suggestions later in this book about market research and proof of concept will also help you become more accurate in determining value, but only when you've considered all the variables and crunched the numbers can you determine a fair dollar value of ownership. While there may be no exact set of formulas that I or any other writer could provide that will be helpful, the important thing is that you put forth the effort to figure it out. As crass as it sounds, equating her contribution to dollars is the only way to prevent an unbalanced partnership and feelings of animosity down the road.

I also recommend having a buyout clause in any partnership agreement whenever possible. If someone is bringing value into your business, give yourself an option to buy the ownership back within a fixed time frame. It can be expensive, but not as expensive as giving up a stake in your company indefinitely or possibly being stuck in a partnership that doesn't work. For example, let's say you have a partner who is coming to the table to help manage the logistics and financial operations of your business (a scenario I see often). You determine that, based on the hours and expertise he is contributing, his effort is worth a 25% stake in your business. If you forecast 25% to be worth $100,000 in five years if you reach your corporate goals, present an option to reserve the right to buy that 25% for $50,000 in three years and negotiate from there.

You may be reading this and already have a partner or partners. Perhaps you jointly developed the business idea and have been in it together from day one. I have seen too many of the "we're in this together" partnerships struggle because of the lack of setting expectations that equate to ownership interest. Without fail, it always seems as if one person, sometimes more, feels like she is carrying the majority of the weight. You can avoid that animosity by setting expectations within the partnership group. Identify the needs and challenges of the business that the owners must be responsible for, and make sure you're all in agreement on who is responsible for what. Then, check in regularly with each other and make sure these things are getting done.

What I'm really suggesting is that you think of yourself and your partner(s) as employees. You all work for the same company. If you set this precedent from day one, it will help alleviate partnership issues and set the standard for all future members of your team. Seth, a friend and business advisor with whom I've collaborated for several years, taught me the importance of building an *organizational chart* before ever launching a company, even if you're the sole member of the company. He showed me how every company will have 15-20 different positions the day it launches. The only way to effectively establish balance in an organization, and a partnership, is to define and fill these positions. I've taken his advice for several years, and it has proven to be so effective that I implement it with nearly every client I work with.

As I have implemented this, I've discovered that almost every company can fit into a simple structure of three divisions: business development, product, and operations. However, I typically see organizational charts with people and departments that are all over the map. Simplifying a structure into three divisions accomplishes three things: First, it gives you and everyone in your organization a visual reminder of the basic operations of the business. Second, it helps you focus on filling positions with the right people instead of hiring the available people and then creating positions around them. Third, it lays a foundation for expansion. I encourage you to try this approach with your company.

So now let's take a look at each of these three divisions:

1. **Business Development.** This is where all things related to growing the business and acquiring customers live. Marketing, advertising, brand management, sales, client procurement, etc.

2. **Product.** As the term implies, this division defines the development and management of what you sell. This division is often subdivided on an organizational chart with the specific name of the product or service you provide.

3. **Operations.** Operations is the machine that powers the running of the company. Bookkeeping, HR, office management, logistics, etc.

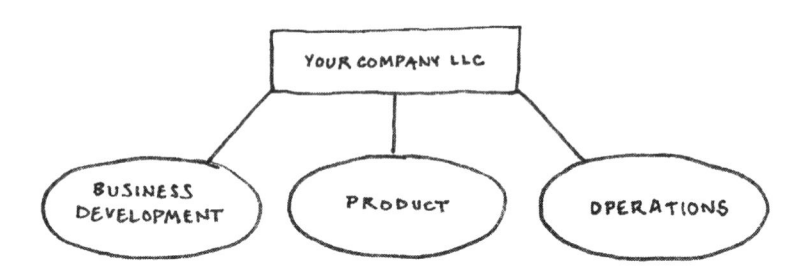

```
                    YOUR COMPANY LLC
                    /      |      \
            BUSINESS    PRODUCT   OPERATIONS
          DEVELOPMENT
```

Now, you can take those three divisions and expand into the specific departments or jobs within each.

Survival Key #3

This next example is based around an apparel business I helped launch. Every one of these positions had to be filled before it went to market. They were filled by three people when it launched—all working part-time.

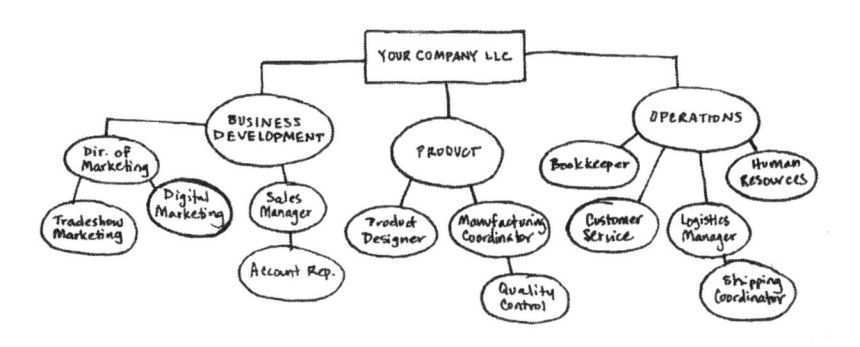

[Organizational chart showing: YOUR COMPANY LLC at the top, branching into Business Development, Product, and Operations. Business Development branches into Dir. of Marketing (Tradeshow Marketing, Digital Marketing) and Sales Manager (Account Rep.). Product branches into Product Designer, Manufacturing Coordinator (Quality Control). Operations branches into Bookkeeper, Customer Service, Human Resources, and Logistics Manager (Shipping Coordinator).]

You can see how quickly a business that seemed like just you working alone out of your basement suddenly looks like a real organization. In the beginning, every position might have your name on it. But by looking at this, you can easily see the jobs that you'll want to fill with someone else as soon as possible.

Beyond personnel expansion, this structure allows for expansion into new product or services categories. Let's say, for example, that we wanted to add a line of watches to our apparel business. That would require new manufacturing processes and relationships. It may also open the door to new markets that we couldn't reach with apparel as our only product offering. The buyers for the jewelry department at a retail store chain might be different than the buyers for apparel, which would require a unique sales and marketing strategy, distinct customer service and possibly even a different team. We'd also want to track financials separately. While the company would still need to maintain its own overarching business development and operations management, each of those product categories would need its own more customized support in those areas as well. The same employees might work in both product divisions, but by creating separation we have a foundation that helps clarify operations and foster expansion.

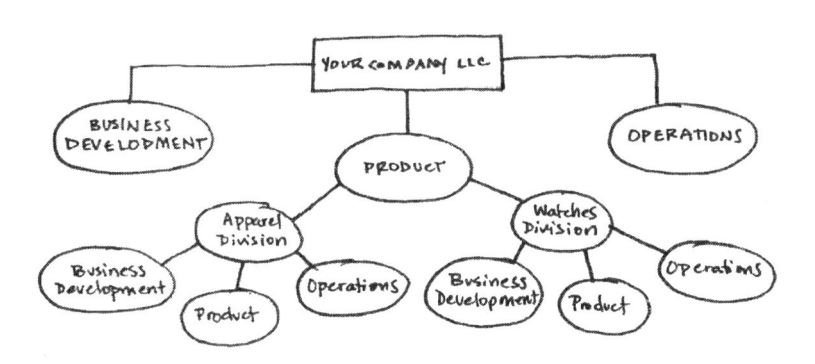

[Organizational chart: Your Company LLC branches into Business Development, Product, and Operations. Product branches into Apparel Division and Watches Division, each with its own Business Development, Product, and Operations.]

Once you've got your structure in place, the second phase of this process is to start creating *job descriptions*. Each position in your org chart has to be supported by the specific expectations associated with it. These will evolve as the company and market evolves, but begin the habit of creating them simultaneously with your organization chart. This will keep you focused and help confirm that you've built your organizational structure around the correct positions (or that you need to make some changes).

Beyond your internal business team, this process can be drawn out to include third parties as well. Some of the roles in your org chart may have to be filled by others. Perhaps your company will need a CFO and you can't afford one today; you'll need to fill that role with an accounting firm until you can justify the expense of a full-time or part-time CFO, but it still fits on the org chart. With the apparel company I referenced above, all of our printing and embroidery was managed by third-party contractors, since the cost to bring that in-house was far greater than we could justify when we started. That is normal in any business.

This entire exercise may seem tedious and might make you cringe. But consider this: studies show that over 95% of all small businesses have no plan for growth. Furthermore, other studies show that 80% of businesses don't survive five years, and over 90% don't last ten years. Perhaps there's a correlation.

Creating an org chart supported by job descriptions is a foundational element to growing a business. You can't effectively build the *who* side of the business, as Jim Collins suggests, without one. As the old saying goes: measure twice, cut once. Save yourself the hassle and expense of fixing the *who* problem later by creating a structure that allows you to get it right today.

There is another side to this equation though: how do you know you've got the right people? Or, how do you find the right people?

There are Human Resource professionals across the world who study this topic and put elaborate, scientific processes in place to analyze people before they hire them. There have also been volumes written on how to train, motivate, and keep employees. Despite all of that, every company on earth has gotten this wrong at least once, most of them multiple times. We are humans: we change, we grow, we have emotions, we get bored, we get lazy, we get ambitious, we get distracted, we win, we lose, we get confused, we fail, we succeed. So no matter what you read, or what anyone tells you, there is no possible way to know you've found or will find the right person for every role in your company. But, that's obviously not a good enough answer, so here are some tips on how find and develop the *right people:*

1. **Do not waiver from your org chart and job descriptions.** Those are built around the purpose, process, and goals of the organization. If an individual's skills, passions, or training do not fit in that

structure, he is not the right person for your company no matter how much you like him.

2. **When you find someone who you think is right to join your company, build her job description around her as an individual.** That may sound like it contradicts what I previously said, but keep in mind that she will probably fill more than one role on your org chart. Incorporate the job descriptions that you've already created for each position, but then match the overarching job description to her. Set expectations for her as an individual, along with those set in the positional description.

3. **Involve the employee in that process.** You might be pleasantly surprised to discover what hidden talents your people have and discover other roles in your company they might be able to fill, even if only for a season. Doing this also reminds them that you value them as individuals and not just as positions. Positions are replaceable. Right people are invaluable.

> *Making people feel replaceable guarantees you will be replacing them.*

Making people feel replaceable guarantees you will be replacing them.

4. **Ask your current and potential team members what they want to accomplish, both in their lives and in their careers with you.** Help them set goals for success in their positions, but also goals for their personal lives that success in their positions can contribute to. If they have goals of taking their families to Disney World, look for opportunities to incentivize them to earn extra income and make that a reality. Your commitment to the right people is revealed in how you commit to their own goals, not just how they help you accomplish yours.

5. **Trust your gut.** There are measurable indicators of a person's character, but none are as strong as how you feel when you're around that person. We are hard-wired to emotionally respond to every person we encounter. Listen to your internal indicators, but also remember that we all have good days and bad. If the résumé says he's a good fit but your initial reaction didn't confirm that, give him a second or third chance.

6. **Review and repeat this process regularly.** Positions evolve and people change. No one likes being left in the dark regarding how he or she is do-

ing or what is expected. Create safe spaces to talk to your people on a regular basis without them having a fear of consequences that could affect their standing with the company. Ask them about how they feel they're doing in their job. Are they confident? How do they feel about the company? Is there anything they'd like to change? How are they doing with their goals, both professional and personal?

Every bit of success you will ever achieve will be because of relationships—partners, employees, and customers. On the flip side, your greatest level of stress will be the result of struggling relationships. The foundation for effective relationships in business is having a structure that is built to attract, develop, and keep the right people. You can't survive without it.

The next key to survival is also about the *right people*, but this time on the other side of the equation: the marketplace.

SURVIVAL KEY #4

Know the Terrain

It's an eleven-mile round trip hike to the confluence of the Colorado and Green rivers inside the 337,000 acre Canyonlands National Park in Southeastern Utah. I've seen a lot of picturesque landscapes in my day, and this one ranks among my favorites. I was there in September of 2016 on a perfect seventy-degree, blue-sky day, and the scattered puffs of clouds set the stage for a perfect hike. As we approached the confluence to relax for an hour over lunch, my friend who lives in the area pointed into the distance beyond the rivers and said, "That area out there is one of the most difficult places in the United States for a person to get to; short of being dropped in by helicopter, it's almost impossible."

The southern part of Utah has become a sanctuary for me. You can't turn your head without having your breath taken away by the scenery, and opportunities for adventure are endless. Best of all, you're just a short hike or bike ride from being away from people! (Something we all need from time to time.) To look out in the distance and see a spot that was nearly unreachable was hard for me to grasp—knowing that there are still places like that in today's world is inspiring. While the challenge of being one of the few to get there is appealing, I take more comfort in knowing that almost no one ever will, including me.

There is a trail leading to that view of the rivers where we stood, but despite a marked trail, getting to that spot is still not exactly a walk in the park. Okay, technically it is a walk in the park, but you get the idea. Hiking it requires climbing over some mildly challenging terrain for five and a half miles each way, and the dry climate can dehydrate you if you're not prepared with enough water. It's also not the kind of marked trail many of us are used to. That part of Utah is mostly rock, so when you get into the many remote areas, there are very few carved paths or signs to direct you. You have to pay close attention to the subtle trail markers (cairns) and at least have some sense of where you're going. One slight left turn when you were supposed to go right, and the untrained tourist could quickly become lost out there, where calling for help isn't really an option.

Survival Key #4

This setting creates a perfect analogy for how entrepreneurs often view the marketplace. When discussing goals in Survival Key #2, I used the example of an entrepreneur who wants to take her product into retail stores across America. That thought process can be compared to parking your car at the welcome center in Canyonlands and walking around the 337,000-plus acres assuming you'll just happen to stumble upon the trailhead somewhere out there. Without knowing where to begin, how to hike the terrain, having a sense of the direction and distance, and knowing how to spot trail markers, you'd quickly become lost, having to work backwards to the beginning and start all over again.

Keep that visual in your mind when you think about the marketplace for your business. Depending on what type of product or business you wish to build, the terrain may be flat with signs along the trails and 10 miles of visibility in every direction, or, it might be that spot out in the distance that almost no one has ever been able to get to. Before you can go anywhere in business, you have to develop a keen awareness of the terrain of your particular marketplace.

To help you gain a deeper understanding of how to figure that out, I'm going to outline four factors by which you can analyze your market using one of my clients as an example. These factors, when applied, are what you can use to determine the size and type of business you need to build and the strategies needed to bring it to the market you just defined.

First, a little background. The client I'm referencing is a company called Bloem, founded by my friend Ryan. You may have never heard of them, but at the time of writing this book, approximately one-third of all the plastic flower pots in the United States are manufactured by them each year. Chances are, one of their planters is in your home or on your patio right now. Best of all, they reached that level of success in less than five years.

Bloem as a company (and Ryan as a leader) could be used as a positive example in almost every chapter of this book. I've been privileged to observe and play a small role in the company's growth since it launched. But most of all, they have provided me with a seat in the real world classroom of business. Watching them go from an idea to retail distribution in 10,000 stores throughout North America in five years has been a pretty exciting thing to experience.

As the saying goes: success leaves clues, so let's examine a couple market factors that helped make their success happen.

Defining the Size of the Existing Market

There are millions of flower pots bought by consumers in America every year. When you think about selling products of this nature you have to not only consider the end consumer, but more importantly you have to consider the retail channels that lead to those consumers. It would be accurate to say the marketplace for Bloem is, well, everyone. I've rarely walked into a house that didn't have a flower pot somewhere. But you can't strategize around that fact alone, so further refining their definition of the market had to happen before Bloem could effectively launch. What *could* be calculated was how many big box stores, garden centers, online retailers, and hardware stores were out there that would buy and resell planters. Beyond that, they could easily learn how those retailers liked to purchase and display those types of products.

When launching Bloem, Ryan and his partners could have started a boutique manufacturing company with innovative products that the market had never seen. But was that what the retailers wanted? Or, did they prefer predictability: placing a purchase order with a reputable, stable company that they knew would provide good pricing and service on familiar products?

The answer in this case was a little of both, but primarily the latter. There was certainly room for some design influence in his industry, but the reality was that flower pots had become somewhat of a commodity. Selling a buyer on a new idea, especially as a new company, is never easy. Stability and familiarity were going to be the most important factors if they hoped to get shelf space. They either had to cater to that or try to get around it by selling innovation direct to consumers with hopes of forcing the hand of the retailers—a monumental task to say the least. Either way, their long-term success would be dependent on that retail network. There was no point in second-guessing that fact—the market was defined.

This fact meant that Ryan was going to have to build something bigger than a "one man out of his garage" company so those retailers had confidence that he could deliver the quantity and type of products that they knew would sell based on their data from previous seasons. Stacks of leftover products in the fall was not an option and would have guaranteed a loss of repeat orders.

Transition that to your business. What is the size of your market? The first step in determining your market is defining it around variables you can grasp. Dig deeper and define the actual market you can engage vs. the ambitious market at large. Bloem may become a household name, but that could never happen if they didn't first define the market they could engage. In fact, it wasn't until its fifth year in business, long after defining its retailer market, that

Bloem even began implementing any kind of consumer marketing strategy. An accurate picture of your market is better than a vague one. When you've got that picture you can start to figure out where the space is for you to move within that market, which leads us to the second factor in defining your market.

The Space in the Market

The easiest way to gain a perspective on what the phrase "space in the market" means is to look at competition. Who else is selling in your marketplace? What are they doing well and what are they missing? In the case of flower pots, the product category had gone stale. Buyers were ready to see some gradual innovation, but, as previously referenced, they weren't ready to sacrifice the staple products that had been selling well for many years. The hard sales data may have shown a crowded market with lots of established competition, but there were other factors to consider. I would not define the available space in this market as lack of available product options, but as a lack of luster. The competition was leaving space by failing to recognize the need for more creativity in both product styling and marketing strategies.

Bloem's initial strategy focused around three variables. First, bring retailers a product they knew they could sell. Second, give it fresh energy with new colors and subtle improvements. And third, support it with new branding and marketing strategies. To accomplish this, they negotiated contracts for the distribution or acquisition of existing product lines that the retailers were familiar with. These were well designed products that simply weren't being positioned and marketed as effectively as they could have been. Bloem stepped in and solved that problem by doing simple things like monitoring color trends and how they were impacting other home goods product sales. The retailers saw immediate progress because of how Bloem was giving a relatively stale product category new life, and as a result, their sales increased.

This success led to the acquisitions of the product lines of several other companies, and those companies quickly realized they either had to sell or try to catch up. At the same time, acceptance of Bloem's proprietary products also increased as retailers developed an appreciation for how this new company approached the market. Every year, they continue to bring retailers new ideas on how to display and sell products, making Bloem not just a supplier, but a strategic partner in increasing their bottom lines.

In some cases, a business introduces an innovative new product and the market is so wide open it's hard to even define. In other words, that business is the pioneer and there's no one else taking up space. In Bloem's case, they were a business that ventured into an already-crowded market and needed to creatively find the spaces that had been ignored.

Examining the space in the market helps you define whether you're a "me-too" product or an innovative product. Is the market wide open and unestablished, or are you jumping into a very crowded space? Just having a great idea is not enough to get attention. You have to identify the gaps that allow you to get attention. Those gaps may be in innovation, presentation, or operation; or any combination of those.

This is one of my favorite parts of growing a business, because it demands a balance of strategy and creativity. On the one hand, you have to look at the numbers and understand the math behind what the market is doing. On the other you have to be creative enough to figure out how to capture and appeal to human emotion and preference, something that can't be put on a balance sheet.

The Potential Size of the Market

One of the nice things about the flower pot business is that the potential market size is fairly predictable. While there will always be room for expansion, calculating the number of retail stores, end consumers, and planters to be sold in a given year is not that difficult. Despite early growth, Bloem did not make the common mistake of over-building with unnecessary overhead and overly optimistic investments. At the same time, there would be global potential for their products, so they made sure to not limit their abilities. They built a foundation for global growth without "betting the farm," so to say.

In a less predictable emerging industry this can be much more difficult. I worked with a technology start-up during the time when mobile apps were in their infancy. This particular company was working with close-proximity geo-location technology. Predicting the potential market for emerging technology can be a lot of fun. The world of mobile devices and apps opened the door to a level of imagination trumped only by the introduction of the Internet itself. The problem, due to the youth of the technology, was that there was limited data to calculate market behavior. Compare that with the decades of data for something like a flowerpot. Big box stores can calculate almost to the unit how many flowerpots they will sell each season, but it would take years to make an honest assessment of the long-term potential for a particular mobile app. How and where to invest time and resources is only limited by the imagination. But you can't build a business on imagination; you need to build it on educated calculations to the best of your ability.

To do that and calculate the potential market size, one must view it through the eyes of more specific vertical markets—both from calculating revenue potential and for developing take-to-market strategies. If the term vertical market is a new one to you, it essentially means dividing your customer base by specific categories. In the case of the geo-location start-up, we started looking at what we felt were the most probable applications. Municipal areas, recreational trails and parks, large outdoor entertainment facilities and amusement parks, and massive indoor facilities like convention centers were among the first vertical markets. From there, we started working each vertical through a research process to define more specific verticals within them so we could more accurately target our market beta testing (the last stage of testing a technology that includes allowing certain customers to download and test a product before an official release) and develop marketing strategies.

The best way to calculate and anticipate market potential is to fully understand the behaviors of a specific vertical market with other products or product categories. It's a great place to start if you're caught in the guessing game of "how much can we actually sell?" The tendency for an aspiring entrepreneur is to overestimate how many people will actually buy the product or service being offered. The number is usually based on how many people *you think should* buy it, but in reality, multiple barriers to the customer making the purchase must be overcome. For example, despite the $0.99 price tag for mobile apps when they first hit the market, many consumers took more time contemplating that decision than they did spending $80 a month for cable television service. It took the market time to accept people buying mobile apps as a part of their daily life, whereas in many households the thought of not having one hundred plus TV channels would be the equivalent of taking away indoor plumbing.

The best way to overcome the common mistake of overestimating your market potential is to be very customer-centric and specific with your predictions and strategies. The more accurate your vertical market estimates, the more accurate your total market predictions become. Instead of listing "retail stores" as a market for flowerpots, Bloem divides that into national "big box" stores, independent garden centers, hardware stores, online retailers, and more. Doing that from day one allowed them to tackle the smallest market first: learn how they think, how they buy, how to engage with them, how they responded to new innovations, and then move on to the next.

The Energy to Move in the Market

Roll a snowball down a hill. When it's small, you have to push it and keep packing more snow on it. The snowball lives or dies in your hands. But as it grows, you stop packing snow, then stop pushing, and the snowball starts to gain in size and speed on its own. Now your job shifts to steering it. The snowball will roll over and absorb smaller snowballs and possibly run over a few kids on their sleds if you're not careful.

The bigger a business needs to become, the more energy it takes to gain momentum. But once you gain that momentum, mass starts to take over and the energy-to-mass ratio shifts. You, as a leader, shift from pushing to driving.

In the case of flowerpots, Bloem made sure they could become large enough and move fast enough to meet the demands of the market. That meant they had to have the energy to build that type of company. That energy came in the form of people, financial capital, and vision. Ryan surrounded himself with the right people who understood and bought in to every aspect of his business, from financial management to national sales strategies. They started with a small percentage of the market but made sure they had the capital and capacity to manufacture products and fulfill orders in larger quantities. When their market acceptance grew, they were prepared to answer the question, "Can you meet our quantity and time frame demands?" From there, they put more energy into expanding the product lines so they could capture more shelf space and become a preferred vendor. The snowball rolled down the hill, and they started absorbing other products and companies, but they have never let it roll out of control.

I give my friend Ryan a lot of credit as he has done, and is doing, a lot of things right. But he also had some advantages. He was in an established industry, he had strong connections, and he was properly funded. Before you call him lucky, however, all three of those variables were entirely his own doing. He knew his industry and his market because he worked hard in it as an employee prior to starting his own company. He built relationships that paved the way for bringing the right people on board and acquiring the capital he needed. There was no family inheritance given or pitch competition won. He started small, did the work, and continues to succeed.

You will need these same ingredients to provide energy to your business, and in my experience, this is where most entrepreneurs get stuck. Specifically, the area of capital is the number-one factor I see holding aspiring entrepreneurs back, so we'll hit that topic more in depth as part of Survival Key #6. The takeaway from this example, however, is that most entrepreneurs don't set themselves up to succeed in this area as Ryan did. They're looking for energy from capital before they'll put the energy into the other areas to get the capital. If you find yourself in this situation, first ask yourself: have I really put the energy into setting myself up for interest from investors, or am I putting my energy into asking for money so I can do all that other work later on their dime?

MetLife produced an ad campaign called "Anything But Small" featuring interviews with business owners. In it, they used the tagline: "Of all the words you use to describe your business, small isn't one of them." That is a brilliant and accurate message. Regardless of what you learn about the size of your market, you need to treat your business as a massive endeavor. However, at the same time, markets don't lie. While it's a big business to you, you must know your customer and know your potential, and you must accurately identify opportunities and calculate how much energy it's going to take to gain traction. It takes effort, just like it takes effort to find your way from the welcome center in Canyonlands to where the rivers merge.

Learn the size, learn the direction, learn the distance, learn the terrain. Have you done that with your market? Have you defined it in size, space, potential, and have you determined the energy it will take to move?

SURVIVAL KEY #5

Prove Your Concept

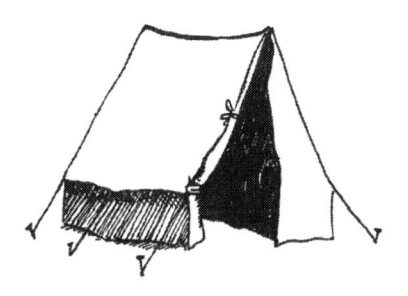

True to my passion as a lover of all things outdoors, I used to be a partner in an outdoor equipment business. We didn't want to create just a "me-too" company, because there was no shortage of outdoor equipment retailers in our town. To reference the previous chapter, at first glance, there did not appear to be much space in the market. However, everyone else in our local market offered one option for that equipment: buy it new. Michigan, where I have lived most of my life, is a beautiful state, but also one where most people only use outdoor gear like kayaks, paddle boards, and mountain bikes for half of the year at best. In the off season (and on the off days) all this gear just takes up space and collects dust in garages and basements across the state. This fact, combined with the upfront purchase cost of the gear, keeps many consumers from enjoying the activities at all.

So we knew we had to be different. Our business model was not to offer another place to buy the gear. We created a business based on renting the gear and marketed it as "your second garage." We offered daily and hourly rental rates, and even a membership package that allowed customers to take gear whenever they wanted for a flat monthly rate, similar to how a health club functions.

I had shared the "health club for outdoor gear" concept with hundreds of people and received the same response across the board: "that's a brilliant idea." Ironically, however, very few of them ever showed up in our store. The business had some success, but for various reasons it never really took off. What seemed like a brilliant solution to a real problem for a lot of people didn't get them off the couch to start kayaking.

It's likely that part of the problem was location. First, we were in a location that's very seasonal. Second, our available capital only allowed for two locations, so if someone wanted to use the equipment elsewhere they would have to transport it. We probably also could have been more aggressive with our marketing, but I think the bigger reason for not getting the traction we anticipated is that while it seemed like a cool idea, the vast majority of people in our community didn't really want to participate in those activities. They liked the *idea* of outdoor activities, but they weren't motivated to actually get off the couch and do it.

To gain market acceptance, we would have had to market the entire concept of getting outdoors more. The reality was that those who wanted to be active and outdoors were already doing it, and for the most part were buying their own gear.

Lesson learned: Cool ideas don't always equal good businesses.

There was another side to this business, however. An afterthought, actually. When we bought our initial inventory of outdoor rental gear, one of my partners suggested we consider buying a few rental campers as well. "Why not?" I thought. I'm sure there are people that would rent those. And they did. In fact, with next to zero marketing around camper rentals, we found ourselves turning down hundreds of customers the first few seasons because we didn't have the inventory to keep up.

One idea seemed brilliant and innovative, the other was just an afterthought. The cool idea didn't end up being a good business (despite every fiber of my being wanting to push the outdoor rental equipment membership program). The afterthought idea wasn't as exciting, but it proved to work.

What we did in that period of time was one of the most critical steps in launching any business: **proof of con-**

cept. Write those words down and never forget them. It is the most important step you take with any idea or new business. Proof of concept is the backbone of engaging the market and having access to the capital needed to expand an idea into a business.

Because I'd proven that the camper rental idea worked, I could easily and instantly get capital with a simple phone call to buy more campers. I couldn't get that capital to buy rental kayaks. I could grow a camper business to hire employees and provide myself profits. I could expand it across the state and country if I wanted to. All because my partners and I proved that the concept works, and had figured out how to run it.

Proving a concept is essential, but it can be difficult for a few reasons. It can be expensive, requiring a significant sacrifice of your time and resources. To reiterate an earlier point, entrepreneurship and risk go hand in hand. The process of proving a concept is where that risk really starts to manifest.

It appears to me that fewer and fewer entrepreneurs now are willing to take risks with their own time and money. In the decade prior to writing this book there was a cultural shift in entrepreneurship. Pitch competitions and start-up events around the United States created a perception that investment capital in a business is some kind of prize to be won; like American Idol for entrepreneurs. While I appreciate how investors and organizations are trying to stimulate growth and innovation, I fear that this mindset does not prepare entrepreneurs for the real world of business. Risk is one of your greatest assets as an entrepreneur, and trying to circumvent it will hurt you.

The cultural shift made many entrepreneurs believe that getting capital should be the first goal, when in reality your first goal should be proving a concept, taking the necessary calculated risks yourself. Then, go get the capital. I have seen countless aspiring entrepreneurs run around with mediocre business plans for months and years because they are chasing money first. I would go as far as to say that you have no businesses asking for a penny of someone else's money until you've proven, to the best of your ability, that you've got something worth investing in. I can't make this point strongly enough: do not get stuck in the chasing money game. Take the risk and prove your concept has market validity.

There are five different elements I use as my foundation for proving a concept:

1. Prove that the Product or Service Holds Value

Whether you're selling yourself as a consultant, renting campers, or selling mobile apps, the same thing is true across the board: you have to create something that adds value. Every decision a human being makes is based on value—from the time we get up, to what we wear, to who we hang out with. You need to enter your product or service into that narrative and see how it measures up. Can you articulate your value proposition? What is happening in the life of your target market that changes when your product or services enters the picture? What would warrant people spending money on whatever it is you offer?

The reason the value proposition was so understandable for camper rentals was because it already played into the behaviors of so many people. Camping is extremely popular in Michigan, so we didn't have to sell people on the idea of camping. But for many, camping would be so much more enjoyable in a nice camper if they could afford it. There are multiple barriers to buying a camper. The obvious one is cost. But beyond that, the cost is relative to the age of the camper. One's budget may not support buying a new camper, but a used camper could require repairs. Beyond that, many people only camp once or twice a year, which makes buying a camper even harder to justify. Add to that the cost of a vehicle to tow the camper and you've got some pretty substantial barriers in place. Enter an affordable, hassle-free solution of renting a camper and having it set up and delivered, and our business was instantly a very appealing option for many campers looking to improve their experience. We quickly identified a very real problem and solved it with a very real solution.

Did proving our concept take risk? You bet. We had to buy the campers, which weren't cheap. We had to store them, insure them, and make sure we had all our ducks in a row to process the rentals and make sure our customers knew how to take care of them. There were several risky logistical variables we had to figure out. For example, if a camper was damaged, we had to cover the expense and deal with the hassle to repair it, not to mention not having that camper for the next renter. But once we figured out how to meet those challenges, we knew we had a viable business worthy of more effort and capital investment.

You can prove the tangible value proposition of your product or service by giving customers a chance to experience it.

2. Prove that You've Correctly Identified the Market

The previous chapter was all about discovering your market. The next step is discovering if it truly responds to your product or service.

Going back to the non-camper side of our business, I honestly believed I had accurately defined the market for outdoor rental equipment. My target customers weren't the outdoor fanatics. My market was the people who wanted to enjoy the hobby but couldn't justify buying the gear. They were people on a limited budget who wanted a variety of options. Families with children were also a major target, because they stood to benefit most from the discount on all the gear when factoring multiple people and multiple hobbies. I knew this target market very well and felt confident in how to engage them, but the value wasn't enough for them to make changes to their lifestyle.

After a few years of experimenting, we came to the conclusion that we had either misidentified the market or misidentified the value of our idea. But the only way to learn that was to take the risk and try it. Again, we surveyed people before we launched, and all signs pointed to this being a great concept, yet in practice it didn't take off. Had we only gone as far as the market surveying and had not tried to prove the concept, we would have invested hundreds of thousands of dollars into that business, and lost big. Instead, we invested a more modest amount on a limited market to test our concept. From there, we knew we could adjust one of three things: our product offering, our market, or how we engaged that market.

In this case, proof of concept didn't spur us on to expansion like it did with campers, it saved us from disaster. We had not correctly identified a market for our idea.

3. Prove that You Know how to Engage the Market

You may have a great idea and a clear understanding of who your target market is. But the next step is a huge leap: knowing how you engage that market. We'll unpack this topic more in Survival Key #7, but effectively reaching your target audience is a science all its own.

When implementing a market engagement strategy in your proof of concept phase, it's important to look at the various stories, or narratives, that play to your market. It's very natural to focus your company's narrative around the features and benefits of your product or service, but what people are primarily interested in is their own story, not yours. When I talk to people about hiring me as an advisor or strategist, my experience and skills are important, but what they ultimately care about is how those skills would make their business stronger.

Think about some of the most memorable advertisements you've seen. What makes them effective? Is it the features and benefits of the product or the way it makes you feel? Apple, the king of marketing, introduced the "1,000 songs in your pocket" advertisement for the iPod in 2001. It featured a young man dancing in his chair in front of his computer, listening to music on earbuds. Then you saw him syncing the songs from his computer to the iPod.

Following the download, he stood up and started dancing around his house. Apple wasn't the only one selling MP3 player technology at the time, but they were the only one selling the lifestyle of an MP3 player. The rest is history. The consumer didn't need to know how many megabytes of storage it had, how long the battery would last, or even how it worked. She just needed to understand how her life would be better with an iPod.

That example may or may not relate to your business. The point is that in your proof-of-concept phase, test different narratives with the market. Depending on what your product or service is, your target market may need to know the features and benefits, or they may just need to be drawn into the story. Your job is to figure that out as early as possible. The only way to do that is to put it out there.

In doing that you can also test different mediums for delivering it. This can be another expensive part of proving a concept. Are you getting responses from social ads, search engine marketing, brochures, or traditional media like magazines, billboards, and TV? Are there ways to push word of mouth and viral campaigns? Sponsorships? Experiment with these and track your results.

4. Prove You've Got the Right Pricing

It can be difficult to figure out how much money a new product or service is worth. Thinking back to the previous chapter about flower pots, the price point of those was pretty well established. In that world, your price has to be competitive to gain traction and you're given a starting point. It's not always that easy.

At my company, Navigate, one of the services we offer is web design. I remember one specific time talking to a potential customer who received a quote from a freelance web developer for $3,000 and then one from an established company for $30,000 for the same project. How on earth do you price against that? In the case of a service-based company like Navigate, our product is people's time. We know what that time costs us and what we need to sell it at to break even and be profitable.

If you're entering the marketplace as a web developer, and the market is showing that it supports $3,000 websites, then in your proof-of-concept phase you'll have to determine if you can work at that rate, desire to work at that rate, if you can inch it up, or if you've found the wrong market.

If you're entering the market with something entirely knew and innovative, you're going to have a very different challenge on your hands. There are two factors to consider when pricing something for which there is no comparison. First, know your costs. Survival Key #6 is going to discuss budgets and financial structures, so for the time being just keep this thought in mind: do you really know what it costs to deliver your product or service?

Second, what decisions do your target customers have to make to find room for it in their budget? No matter what you sell, remember that you're always competing with someone. Think about positioning your product or service into their lives, discover the value proposition it holds against other spending habits, and develop your pricing accordingly.

5. Prove Your Ability to Deliver and Scale

Proving you've got a great product, a defined market, an effective engagement strategy, and the right price point is only as valuable as your ability to scale your idea past the proof-of-concept phase. Do you have the right processes in place to grow and create the profitability you need? Can you meet market demands? If you're selling your own time as a service provider, what's the plan for maximizing the limited hours you can sell? Will you add staff?

I've worked with several small product manufacturers over the years who have ambitions for large-scale retail distribution. One of the first questions I ask them is this: If I walked you into retail store X today, and they placed an order for 100 units in each of their stores with delivery in 90 days, can you fulfill it? Most of them obviously cannot. But that's ok because they're not going to get that order right now. But the real question I'm asking is this: do you have a plan for when that day comes? In your proof-of-concept phase you need to develop operational plans for scaling up to the size business you want, based on the market to support it.

Prove your systems and process for product manufacturing and delivery, financial management, time management, logistics, marketing, or whatever else applies to your business. Work out the bugs in the proof-of-concept phase so when time comes to really get rolling, you've anticipated most of the internal challenges you could encounter at a larger scale.

To close out this survival key: I cannot emphasize enough how important proof-of-concept is. There is a term that my friend Michael came up with that I now use on a regular basis when discussing entrepreneurship: "perpetual almost." Perpetual Almost is the entrepreneurial disease of constantly feeling like you've got a great idea but just can't seem to get over the hump. Proof-of-concept is the cure. It will cost you time and money, but if you're intentional about it, it's not time and money lost. Proof-of-concept can literally be the single greatest variable between perpetual almost and successful business owner.

SURVIVAL KEY #6
Do The Math

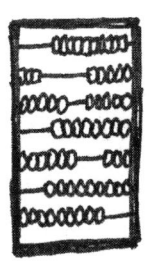

One of the more educational moments in my entrepreneurial career was the first time I pitched an idea to a venture capitalist. This wasn't a family member or friend—it was the real deal. Their office was in a big city high rise and they obviously had their hands in some serious deals. I was in my 20s at the time, I was a bit of a rookie, and I was overwhelmed. After my pathetic attempt at a pitch, I think they were overly generous in not kicking me out. Instead, the company's founder talked me through the various elements of my business plan that I would need to address if I were to ever obtain capital from a company like theirs. The most memorable thing he said to me was, "Rob, I want you to show me down to the coffee straws how much money you're going to spend every month. Not because I really care how much you spend on coffee straws, but if you ever want us to invest, we need to know that *you* care how much you spend on coffee straws."

The simple, yet profound lesson he taught me was this: business is math. Business always comes down to the numbers, and if you're not going to pay attention to the numbers, don't get into business. And certainly don't ask someone else to take a financial risk on you. Ignoring the numbers has cost me more than anything else in my career. When I look back at the real reasons for my career crash, it all comes back to the math. I didn't understand the numbers and didn't pay attention to them. I didn't want to. I'm not wired to sit at a desk looking at Quickbooks and spreadsheets. I'm relational and outgoing, which is great for being a salesman, not a CFO. So I delegated the task of crunching the numbers to others. The decision to assume the finances were being handled by someone else was the worst decision of my career.

> *If you're not going to pay attention to the numbers, don't get into business.*

It's easy to justify spending your time on what you're good at and finding others to carry the load of the things you're not good at. For the most part, that's ok and I encourage it. But when it comes to the numbers, you have no choice. Whether you own 1% or 100% of the business, you cannot delegate your personal responsibility as an owner to understand the math. Others can facilitate the process and produce reports, but you need to be on top of it daily. I have forced myself to become diligent in this behavior and have even found that I like it more than I ever thought I would (especially when the numbers are headed in the right direction).

The process of doing the math as an entrepreneur starts before you launch. You may be wondering what kind of math can really be done if there's no money coming in and no money going out. Similar to building the organization chart when you're the only person in your organization, you need to start planning the numbers when all you have is a dream and a personal checking account.

That process starts by learning to create a financial Pro-Forma. If you're not familiar with that term, it essentially refers to a method for tracking and predicting the financial state of the business, including forecasts as far out in the future as is realistically possible. Think of it as a more in-depth version of a budget, just like you might have for your personal finances.

I learned to create ProFormas several years ago in a spreadsheet format—a habit you can adopt without help from accountants or accounting software. On the left of the spreadsheet I list my fixed operating expenses, my payroll and related expenses, and my revenue estimates. Across the top of the spreadsheet are the months from left to right—I recommend looking at least twelve months ahead. Then, write your formulas. I include a formula for a cash-flow summary that carries the previous months profits over into the next month. Once the framework is in place, you can start plugging in numbers. On the opposite page is an example of a very basic twelve-month ProForma for the small apparel company start-up used for the org chart example in chapter 3.

While a CPA may cringe at its simplicity, going through this process provides several benefits to you as the entrepreneur.

First, doing a ProForma yourself versus having someone else do it forces you to think through the numbers. The first ProForma I ever saw was completed by a CPA. It was far more impressive than what I could have created, but not being an integral part of creating it deprived me of the thought process that went into it. I didn't fully understand it or embrace it. Now, I do just the opposite. I start with my own ProForma and then give it to the CPAs as a starting point for their work.

Second, it helps set goals. Knowing your company's revenue projections and profitability gives you a founda-

Survival Key #6

Example of a Twelve-Month ProForma:

EXPENSES	January	February	March	April	May	June	July	August	September	October	November	December	TOTALS
Operating													
Office Space / Utilities	$450.00	$450.00	$450.00	$450.00	$450.00	$450.00	$450.00	$450.00	$450.00	$450.00	$450.00	$450.00	*$5,400.00*
Misc. Supplies	$1,000.00	$150.00	$150.00	$150.00	$150.00	$150.00	$750.00	$150.00	$150.00	$150.00	$150.00	$150.00	*$3,250.00*
Legal / Accounting	$1,000.00	$350.00	$350.00	$350.00	$350.00	$350.00	$350.00	$350.00	$350.00	$350.00	$350.00	$350.00	*$4,850.00*
Software / Web Hosting	$140.00	$140.00	$140.00	$140.00	$140.00	$140.00	$140.00	$140.00	$140.00	$140.00	$140.00	$140.00	*$1,680.00*
Merchandise													
Initial Inventory / Samples	$2,500.00	$2,500.00	$0.00	$0.00	$0.00	$0.00	$0.00	$0.00	$0.00	$500.00	$0.00	$0.00	*$5,500.00*
Screen Printed Apparel	$0.00	$600.00	$900.00	$1,800.00	$2,400.00	$3,000.00	$3,600.00	$4,500.00	$5,400.00	$7,500.00	$12,000.00	$12,000.00	*$53,700.00*
Embroidered Apparel	$0.00	$650.00	$975.00	$1,950.00	$2,600.00	$3,250.00	$3,900.00	$4,875.00	$5,850.00	$8,125.00	$13,000.00	$13,000.00	*$58,175.00*
Marketing / Sales													
Trade Shows	$0.00	$0.00	$2,000.00	$2,000.00	$0.00	$0.00	$0.00	$0.00	$0.00	$0.00	$3,000.00	$0.00	*$7,000.00*
Digital Ads / S.E.M	$500.00	$500.00	$500.00	$1,000.00	$1,000.00	$1,000.00	$1,000.00	$1,000.00	$1,000.00	$1,000.00	$3,000.00	$3,000.00	*$14,500.00*
Print Ads	$0.00	$0.00	$0.00	$0.00	$0.00	$0.00	$0.00	$0.00	$1,000.00	$1,000.00	$1,000.00	$1,000.00	*$4,000.00*
Travel	$0.00	$250.00	$1,000.00	$1,000.00	$250.00	$250.00	$250.00	$250.00	$250.00	$250.00	$1,500.00	$250.00	*$5,500.00*
Payroll													
Manager Salary	$0.00	$0.00	$0.00	$0.00	$0.00	$0.00	$0.00	$0.00	$0.00	$0.00	$0.00	$0.00	*$0.00*
Logistics Coordinator	$0.00	$0.00	$0.00	$0.00	$0.00	$750.00	$1,000.00	$1,000.00	$1,000.00	$1,500.00	$1,500.00	$1,500.00	*$9,000.00*
Marketing Coordinator	$0.00	$0.00	$500.00	$500.00	$500.00	$500.00	$500.00	$500.00	$500.00	$500.00	$500.00	$500.00	*$5,000.00*
Trade Show Help	$0.00	$0.00	$300.00	$300.00	$0.00	$0.00	$0.00	$0.00	$0.00	$0.00	$500.00	$0.00	*$1,100.00*
Total Expenses	$5,590.00	$5,590.00	$7,265.00	$9,640.00	$8,590.00	$9,840.00	$11,940.00	$13,215.00	$16,090.00	$21,465.00	$37,090.00	$32,340.00	*$178,655.00*
REVENUE ESTIMATES													
Screen Printed Apparel Sales	$0.00	$1,000.00	$1,500.00	$3,000.00	$4,000.00	$5,000.00	$6,000.00	$7,500.00	$9,000.00	$12,500.00	$20,000.00	$20,000.00	*$89,500.00*
Embroidered Apparel Sales	$0.00	$1,000.00	$1,500.00	$3,000.00	$4,000.00	$5,000.00	$6,000.00	$7,500.00	$9,000.00	$12,500.00	$20,000.00	$20,000.00	*$89,500.00*
Total Revenue	$0.00	$2,000.00	$3,000.00	$6,000.00	$8,000.00	$10,000.00	$12,000.00	$15,000.00	$18,000.00	$25,000.00	$40,000.00	$40,000.00	*$179,000.00*
Net Profit Total	-$5,590.00	-$3,590.00	-$4,265.00	-$3,640.00	-$590.00	$160.00	$60.00	$1,785.00	$1,910.00	$3,535.00	$2,910.00	$7,660.00	*$345.00*
Running Cash-flow	-$5,590.00	-$9,180.00	-$13,445.00	-$17,085.00	-$17,675.00	-$17,515.00	-$17,455.00	-$15,670.00	-$13,760.00	-$10,225.00	-$7,315.00	$345.00	

tion for knowing how many customers you'll need and what margins you need to hit.

Third, creating a ProForma shows potential partners and investors that you've done the research and know what it will take to make money. Investors want to see that you've thought this through and haven't just taken a guess.

Fourth, after you're up and running, it's something you can refer back to and update regularly. Your ProForma becomes a working budget that you can compare to your actual month-end numbers and edit accordingly.

Finally, your ProForma becomes the foundation for a business plan. You can't just pull the numbers out of thin air; you have to explain how you got to those numbers. If you say you're going to do $10,000 in revenue next month, what is that based on? How many customers and at what dollar amount? How are you getting those customers? Both you and potential investors need to know that. The result of building and maintaining ProFormas and budgets is that you can create a *Working Business Plan* versus just a *Hypothetical Idea Plan*. Once you've got your financial picture established, you can start looking at what it's going to take to prove your concept and take it to market. You can calculate the risk instead of just guessing at a dollar amount you need to launch.

Survival Key #6

Though it is not popular advice among many aspiring entrepreneurs, my advice to you is to look at your numbers and commit to taking on as much of the financial risk yourself as possible, especially in the proof-of-concept phase. I intentionally created the ProForma example with no management salary to make a point: don't plan on making money your first year in business. You might make some money, but don't plan on it. That's part of the risk. Second, look at that lowest point of running cashflow, which in the example ProForma is -$17,675.00. If your numbers are relatively accurate, that's the amount of investment you need. If I were actually launching this business I would want to pad it a little and have $20,000 in the account before I opened the doors.

Your ProForma may show you need thousands of dollars or millions. Regardless, the best thing you can do for yourself and potential partners is to take as much of it on yourself as possible. Obviously, the more risk you take, the less ownership you give up. But there's a more important reason to invest in your business yourself.

Allow me to elaborate by asking you a question: if you were in the market for a new car, how much time would you spend calculating the investment if I bought it for you rather than you buying that car yourself? If you're being honest, you'll calculate the investment in a new car with far more detail and time when it's your own money. Why?

Because there's more pain associated with letting go of something you've worked for, and as a result you will try to make better spending decisions. I promise you will push the salesperson for a better price if you're spending your money versus mine. The farther the spender is from the earner, the worse the decision-making gets (i.e. government spending).

The more personal the investment risk is to you, the closer you'll pay attention to the numbers. And your business always needs you to pay attention to the numbers. Even if you're investing the least amount of all your business partners, the sacrifice you make sends a message to everyone involved, including yourself, that you are committed and can be trusted with the decision-making of the company. On the flip side, asking investors to accept 100% of the financial risk, especially if you're including a nice paycheck for yourself, is one of the biggest red flags they look for. Show them that you have skin in the game. If you do the work to get accurate numbers, you may be pleasantly surprised to discover how little money you may actually need and how realistic it is to have that skin in the game.

It might feel impossible to front any of the investment yourself. It is common to want to (and feel that you have to) get capital before getting an idea off the ground. But nothing could be further from the truth. Capital does not solve everything. It's a tool, but it is only valuable if you fully understand the amount of capital you need and the right source from which to get it. When I was in my 20s, I believed all I needed was money to make my plan work. But in all honesty, if you had thrown ten million dollars at me 20 years ago, I still would have failed. If I couldn't manage a checking account with a hundred dollars in it, how could I possibly handle one with a million dollars in it?

The next problem, the source of the money, can be a little tougher to accept. Many entrepreneurial-minded people seem to forget that you can get capital every two weeks by going to work. It's contrary to the entrepreneurial nature to go and get a job. Believe me, I understand that as well as anyone. We see the days ticking by and feel like our moment will pass if we don't act now. But if your idea is good enough, and you're equipped to build it, you have nothing to worry about. If you're concerned about competition stealing your idea if you wait too long, you're just proving to yourself and everyone else that you don't believe enough in your idea to outdo your competition; or you don't believe enough in your ability to lead the charge. In either case, you probably shouldn't be seeking capital from anyone else at this point.

Some of the best advice my friend Greg gave me back in 2008 when I was hitting the reset button on my career was to live cheap and get a job. I took his advice, and here's how it played out:

We downsized houses and moved into a rental house that cost $600 a month and was in need of some work. I drove a rusty pickup with 170,000 miles on it, and my wife drove an old sedan with 330,000 miles on it. Both cars were gifts from sympathetic family members. We bought clothes from thrift stores, and the only vacation we took was a generous Christmas gift from a family member. It was extremely humbling to go from renovating a 6,000-square-foot home on a lake to an old rental home, from an S-Class Mercedes to a rust bucket. At times, it was embarrassing. I often wanted to park my truck three blocks away from a meeting location so no one would see me walk to it. But I was also proud of myself knowing that I was no longer my own worst enemy. Not wanting to stay in that place also motivated me.

Then, I got a job. I committed to at least one year of doing nothing but working, earning, and saving. I had tons of ideas spinning in my mind during that year, but I let them sit. After that year, I started to think about new business ventures. But I didn't rush into anything. This one-year commitment actually turned out to be a period of several years where I went from full-time employment to part-time while I restarted the entrepreneurial process.

Because I wasn't in a hurry to start a business, I had time to simply live life and observe what was around me. I was able to watch the market and identify opportunities. Instead of being obsessed with a single cool idea, I was able to look for problems I could solve and in the process discover opportunities where my ideas and skill set could produce a viable business. Through this, I slowly started to really develop an idea that I thought had potential.

I didn't rush the idea, and I didn't rush the finances. With a few years of working and saving, my bank account had grown. In what seemed like the blink of an eye, I was in a position to launch a business. Instead of running around asking for money, I was able to move forward, putting a plan into action on my own. I had a plan, I had my own money and time into it, and I was moving forward. I began having casual conversations about my business plan, and all of a sudden I had people approaching me about investing. And I never had to pitch my idea, not once.

Whether you've crashed and burned and are rebuilding (like I did), or you're starting fresh, the lesson is the same: get your house in order. Try the old-fashioned way for a little while and see what happens. Live cheap. Work hard. Save money. You might be pleasantly surprised at how far you can get on your own, and, how much more appealing you suddenly become to investors.

Now, assuming after all that you will still need some capital, consider this:

Has anyone ever told you that investors will invest in you and not your idea? It's a commonly taught principle, which is completely true but often misunderstood. At first glance one could easily assume that phrase implies something about investing in a person's character and integrity. While there's an element of truth to that, it's only a small part of what that statement means.

All investors, private or institutional, invest in your track record more than your personality. They want to mitigate their own risk, and they expect you to share in the risk. They invest in you based on how well you manage yourself, not whether or not you are a nice person. Banks want credit reports, personal financial statements, and personal guarantees. Why? Because they are investing in your track record of how you handle money. When your business becomes established and has its own track record, they'll transition their focus accordingly. But in the early days, they're looking at you.

Investment is a financial transaction based on formulas and risk assessment. Allow me to go ahead and beat this point to death: get your personal finances in order. Then, get your business numbers dialed in.

To bring this entire chapter full circle, doing the math never stops. It's not just something you do to get capital. Every day of your life as a business owner must involve number crunching. Profit is the reason you start a business, and cashflow is the lifeblood of every business. If you don't take that seriously enough, you might as well call it a hobby. To be profitable demands never-ending attention to the numbers that get you there.

SURVIVAL KEY #7

Create Movement

My first real "grown-up" job was as a sales rep for a commercial audio visual company. We designed and installed large sound, video, and lighting systems in places like churches, schools, and sporting venues. I had some success early on, and gained the attention of one our competitors. The owner of that competitive company invited me out boating with him to talk about me joining his team—knowing I was a boater, taking me out on his much larger boat was certainly a wise tactic to get my attention. While I was flattered by the offer to work for him, I was more curious about why. He had the more established company and more cash, and he had weathered far worse storms in business than some young hot-shot sales guy winning a few projects. His answer has stayed with me for years: "Rob, nothing happens until something gets sold."

Despite the decades of experience, established processes, long-standing employees, substantial client list, buying power, and every other advantage he had over us, he knew none of it mattered if he couldn't get people signing contracts and writing checks. In his 30+ years of experience, he had realized that if there was any position in his company he had to pay close attention to and invest in, it was the sales position. So, when he saw someone who had a knack for that, he jumped at the opportunity

> *Nothing happens until something gets sold.*

"Nothing happens until something gets sold" is actually a re-wording of Albert Einstein's famous quote, "Nothing happens until something moves." When talking business, that's what sales really is: movement. It's taking everything you've dreamed about, strategized, tested, and funded, and giving it some movement in the marketplace.

We've talked about the landscape of the marketplace, and in the proof-of-concept phase we've had some interaction with it, but now we're going to truly immerse ourselves in the marketplace with our marketing and sales strategies. How do we actually get the attention of that target market?

Marketing is the hardest check for any business owner to write because it's nearly impossible to accurately measure a return on investment. However, it's really easy to calculate the effects of not marketing. To help make that investment a little more palatable, I teach a five-step process called "The Five M's." When applied, this process can help you avoid the syndrome of "throwing mud against the wall"—an all-too-common, and expensive, approach to marketing. The five steps are:

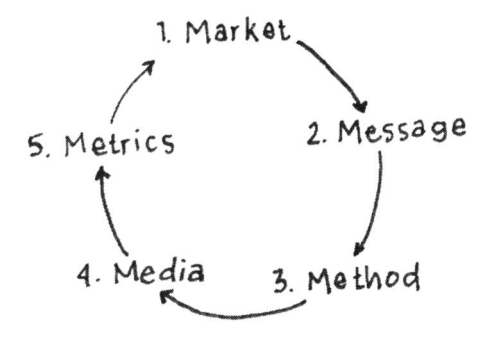

1. Market
2. Message
3. Method
4. Media
5. Metrics

M #1: Market

We already hit this topic in Survival Key #4, but there is a transition that happens between understanding your market and engaging your market. As you take an idea to market you'll realize that there are different sub-demographics that latch onto your business in a certain order. Although they may all fit in the same general demographic of your greater marketplace and more specific vertical markets, they still have different personality types and decision-making habits. There is a commonly taught way to organize those people into five categories, called the Innovation Adoption Curve, initially made popular by writer and professor, Everett Rogers.

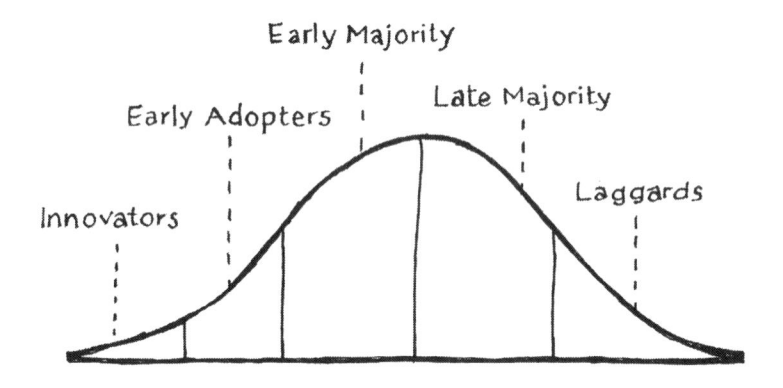

Bell curve diagram labeled, from left to right: Innovators, Early Adopters, Early Majority, Late Majority, Laggards.

Using this curve will help you determine how to focus your energy and investment. You'll discover specific patterns that help you understand what types of people fit where so you know who to engage first and how.

Innovators are people like you. They were with you in the early stages, helping develop and test, and are hopefully telling all their friends about what's happening.

Early Adopters are those who want to be a part of the next big thing before everyone else. They want the inside scoop and love being the person to tell everyone else about something new. They think of themselves as trend-setters because they saw something happening before the rest of the market. They're ahead of the curve, willing to take risks just to be the first. They wait in line for product releases. They're excited by innovation. They read the articles and follow the experts.

Early Majority are the ones who want some sort of market response before they'll buy something. They're going to read reviews or ask for testimonials. This is where you'll want to invest a lot of your marketing energy. Take the excitement of the *Early Adopters* and use it as fuel and proof-of-concept to engage this large segment of your marketplace.

Late Majority are the ones who hesitate. If everyone else is doing it, they guess they'd better too. They need to feel more confident before they make a purchase. They wait until the bugs have been worked out.

Laggards may or may not ever buy into what you're selling. If they do, they can often be the first to find something wrong so they can justify why they didn't jump in early. They'll research every alternative first.

At first, this innovation/adoptive cycle may feel like it only applies to new innovation (as the name implies), but it can be applied to any business, or even a new marketing strategy. The way people tend to respond to innovation is reflective of how they respond to almost any decision. Are they quick to jump in, or do they need to feel 100% confident before making a decision? As a service provider, I have put nearly identical contracts in front of multiple people. Some listen to me talk and sign without reading. Others read it and come back with 20 questions. While I'm not offering anything that could be labeled very innovative, they still fit into that curve. The longer I do this, the quicker I learn to identify who fits where so I can relate to them accordingly.

For that to be effective, however, you need to first embrace the simple understanding that the marketplace is made up of emotional human beings. For all the number crunching and analyzing I've recommended that you perform, it can never trump the fact that the decision for someone to purchase or not purchase is an emotional one. People choose a product, service, or person based as much on how they feel as much as how well they understand. When doing some research for Bloem (the flower pot company) a few years ago regarding the impact of product color on marketing and display strategies, we came across a study by Satyendra Singh from the University of Winnipeg which stated: *People make up their minds within 90 seconds of their initial interactions with either people or products.* About 62–90 percent of the assessment is based on colors alone.

How can you possibly quantify what to do with that? For Bloem, that information helped them shape their product strategy. Color may have nothing to do with your product or service, but the point is that human emotion and personal preference are significant factors in why people make decisions, possibly the most significant factors. You can't sell yourself, or a product, in 90 seconds solely on features and benefits. Your strategies for market engagement have to cater to human emotion.

In the book *Insanely Simple: The Obsession That Drives Apple's Success*, author Ken Segall provides a contrast between the advertising strategies of Apple and other competitive computer companies. Having worked for both, he offers a unique perspective on the subject. One of the many conclusions I derived from the book was that both Apple's advertising and product offerings were heavily driven by using the most basic understanding of how people process information. We are storytellers by nature. To be effective in selling someone on an idea or product, one must become a great storyteller. It's hard to engage in a story with dozens of characters. Apple only introduces one or two characters (products) into a story at a time and keeps the narrative of that story extremely relatable, not packed full of information.

At the time of this writing, Apple remains the most profitable company on earth. Why? Are Apple products manufactured better and equipped with better features? Maybe. But I believe their success comes from the fact that both their products and their advertisements are more human than the competition. Their story is our story, not a story of megabytes, warranties, and features. They charge more and sell more because they've tapped into the psyche of how people process information, and have traditionally held that in as high regard as any other factor when taking a product to market. So how do you take that and ingrain it into your business? There are two things I suggest you do:

First, get real human reactions.

Conduct surveys on your product, services, advertising, pricing, options, etc. Not just initially, as we discussed in the proof-of-concept phase, but regularly. Put together your own focus groups and build online surveys that you can push via social channels and email blasts. Get customer feedback, good and bad. If need be, take it a step further and bring in a market research company to guide and facilitate the process. Ask questions related not only to whether people like your idea, but would they actually spend money on it? There's a big difference between someone liking your idea and actually spending money on it, as I explained in my outdoor equipment company example. Ask questions like: Do you currently buy competitive product X? Or do you subscribe to service Y? Or, would you sacrifice spending your money on product X to purchase my product instead?

Remember that no matter how unique your idea is, there's always something out there competing for people's money, or there's something that currently solves the same problem. For example, the invention of the automobile was a better way for people to get from one place to another, but the concept wasn't new. Horses and carriages had existed for generations, so why would someone replace their perfectly good buggy with an expensive, noisy, motorized version of that? Just because it was innovative didn't mean everyone realized it solved a problem for them. Bridging the gap between knowing who your market is, and actually getting them to come your way, means first meeting them where they are today. Then you can try to take them somewhere new tomorrow.

Second: become a great storyteller—which brings us to the second "M."

M #2: Message

Think back to middle school English class, when you were taught how to structure a basic three-act story. Great stories always set the context first. The exposition, as it's often called, helps make everything that follows more understandable. In that first act, you're immersed in the setting and begin to connect with the characters so that when they're introduced to a challenge or obstacle in the story, you're already invested.

Keeping with Apple as an example, let's go back to the iPod ad we talked about in Survival Key #5. The context, or exposition, of that story was a young man listening to songs through earbuds attached to a computer. That was nothing new, but by setting the stage in that way, the viewer immediately understood what was happening. Then, those songs moved to the little magic device next to the computer, which made us realize something exciting was about to happen. Finally, the man started dancing all over his house with those same ear buds in, now free to move and dance as much as he wanted to, all because of that little device in his hand! Suddenly, you want to be that person! 1,000 digital song files in my pocket? I don't care what it's called or how much it costs, I want it! A month later when all your friends have one (early adopters), you're not even sure how you could live without it. You have a crisis on your hands if you don't have an iPod.

Telling a great story may not be your area of expertise. Fortunately, there are talented people in every corner of the globe to help you. Storytelling is the foundation of great marketing and advertising, so any credible marketing expert or agency should be able to show you a résumé of story-based campaigns they have developed and implemented. Interview them, have them present their approach, and get someone on board to help.

M #3: Method

The *method* of market engagement refers to the channels by which you reach someone. For example, if your target demographic is older and didn't grow up using the Internet, they probably still get most of their information from traditional sources like television, newspapers, and magazines. Younger audiences, on the other hand, are using digital social platforms.

There are a few variables to consider when selecting methods, but before going into that, I think it's worth noting that there's nothing new under the sun. The dawn of social media in the 2000s felt like a revolution, and to some extent it was. But when you break it down, it's really just the continuation of a revolution that's been evolving for hundreds of years. From newspapers, to magazines, to radio, to TV, to multi-channel Cable TV, to websites, to search engines, to social media, to … You get the picture. Ever since the dawn of advertising, businesses have had to get better and better at navigating the various channels by which people acquire information.

Information continues to move faster and through more channels. On one hand, this is a marketer's dream.

You can hit people from every direction! Plus, with the more modern communication methods, you can more accurately direct advertisements to consumers based on increasingly specific demographics. With each generation we've created new channels that further segregate us based on our preferences. On the other hand, how to choose what to buy and how much to spend is more complicated today than ever.

So here are some helpful tips:

1. **Remember the humanity of your audience: Know your people, and you'll know where they spend time.** Age and location are the two initial factors you can start with to narrow down the demographics within your target market and select methods accordingly. Do they read newspapers or blogs? Do they listen to the radio or to podcasts? Do they watch television or YouTube? This will help you decide where to market.

2. **The beauty of modern advertising, especially with social channels, is your ability to adjust on daily basis.** While I'm all for traditional advertising on TV and in print media, if you're on any type of a budget, see how much traction you can gain with digital strategies first. Find out who

responds before you invest into longer-term (and more expensive) commitments.

3. **Borrow credibility.** Look for existing organizations and social pages that have already narrowed your market down. This is no different than attending trade shows—you already have your target audience in one giant room! Bloggers, social pages, and media companies all offer opportunities with digital and traditional advertising platforms to position your brand along with theirs.

4. **Participate in what the market cares about.** Attach your brand to charitable causes, community events, and online campaigns that are meaningful to your company and your target audience. Be authentic with this, however, not just opportunistic.

5. **Understand the difference between brand awareness and market messaging.** In Survival Key #9 we'll talk more about your brand, but when implementing any campaign there is a time and place to just simply attach your identity (such as a sponsorship) and a time to deliver a message (such as a social ad or post). Make sure you understand the best use of each method you choose to utilize.

M# 4: Media

The *media* in this case doesn't refer to the news networks, but to the media you create to deliver your *message* to your *market* in the most effective *method*: your marketing and advertising assets. When you've made progress on those three variables, you can start creating the media accordingly. The most common mistake I see in this phase is that it's typically done out of order. I've had many entrepreneurs come to me with what they thought were great marketing assets, yet they wondered why they weren't gaining traction. The problem was that they got excited about designing cool stuff before they knew who they were designing it for, and how they were reaching them.

There are obviously some basic "givens" in marketing. In today's world, whether you're selling products or consulting services, you need a website. Not just any website—a good website that works on any screen size and is easy to navigate. Even app-based businesses have websites; it's the storefront window of the modern generation. I would also add video to the list of givens with the multitude of platforms and high-speed Internet available almost everywhere on earth. Video is proving to be a far more affordable, authentic, and appealing way to deliver a message than ever before. Furthermore, customers are using video hosting sites as search engines for discovering information, not just to be entertained.

Survival Key #7

Beyond those givens, print media still has its place. In fact, in talking with local print companies, I'm continually amazed to hear that their businesses continue to grow despite the online revolution.

The list goes on and on, whether it's sales presentations, social pages, or advertisements, there are some tried-and-true marketing assets that you just need to have. If you make sure this step follows the others, you'll have a much better handle on what you really need before wasting a bunch of money on what you don't need.

So how do you start designing your media? There are two extremely important things to remember:

1. **Get it done right, and hire professionals.** I may be biased because I have a vested interest in a marketing agency, but that's not the point. A professional person or company doesn't just give you a high quality of design or production, they also give you a non-emotional, experienced perspective. That perspective makes sure you're using the right media, and the professionalism makes sure it's built right and is unique to you versus similar to a hundred other businesses.

2. **Always look at the context.** If you're designing a product label and that product is going to be on

shelves in retail stores, have you visited the store to see what else is nearby? What will you be doing to stand out? If you're creating an ad for a local publication, are you going to be one of four ads on the same page? Creating effective media isn't about making something you like, it's about making something that's *magnetic* and *memorable* (apparently I love the letter M). The more you consider context, the more you can make that a reality. No matter what you create, you're competing for attention. We all see thousands of ads every year: TV, social media, online videos, website ads, trade-shows, billboards, and magazines. What will you design to get noticed?

M #5: Metrics

I said earlier that marketing is the hardest check to write because it's very difficult to calculate return on investment. How do you know if a person came to your business because they saw an ad or heard about you from someone else? Or both? Or saw multiple ads? It's truly impossible to know for sure. But what you can do is look at traffic. How many people visit your website, walk in your door, dial your phone, or send you a message?

Pay attention to those numbers. Look at them week to week, month to month, quarter to quarter, and year to year. Then compare that with where you've invested. If your business is strictly online, you can get surprisingly precise with this. There are companies spending millions on infrastructure and analysis to calculate data by the minute. Chances are you're not one of them, but you can adopt their philosophies. The phrase "Business is math" doesn't just apply to your bookkeeping, it applies to your market engagement. Study the data, look for correlations, and adjust accordingly.

Once you've done all of this, it's time to actually go out and sell. So now I'd like to revisit the salesperson role. If your business depends on actual sales people versus relying solely on marketing strategies, it's important that you hire people who embrace the same philosophies I just outlined for marketing. They (and/or you) need to mentally go through the same process: Who are the people I'm looking to sell to? What messages will resonate with them? What methods do I need to incorporate to connect with them? What media do I need to support me? And what metrics will I use to measure my effectiveness?

My experience is that good salespeople embrace two qualities:

1. **They are extremely skilled in relationship building.** They are natural conversationalists. They listen, remember, and genuinely care about whom-

ever they're talking to. They also believe that they have something to contribute to the relationship. They want to add value and, furthermore, need affirmation that they are adding value. They want all of their relationships to last, not just be transactional.

2. **They are motivated by closing the deal.** This is different than someone who pushes to close a deal. Great salespeople gain a certain amount of self worth by the acceptance they feel when someone says yes. You can teach anyone to close a sale, but the people you'll want representing you long-term need to possess that inner drive. Yes, money is a good motivator, but it's more personal than that. Great sales people want referrals—they understand that their character is ultimately their product, and the entire process has meaning to them.

There's one final point I want to make about sales, and it's the toughest for any salesperson to accept. My business partner Jeff told me several years ago that he's made most of his money off the things he said no to. I shudder to think about how much money I've lost by saying yes, and doing business with the wrong clients: those that didn't really understand the business model, those who didn't pay their bills, those who were financially or emotionally unstable, or those who were simply never satisfied. One of the keys to success is realizing that you're not right for everyone. The sales process should not be a one-way process. Make sure you're sold on your clients or customers as much as they're sold on you.

There's a lot to this survival key about people. People and relationships are what keeps every business going. They are what take you to the pinnacles of success and what sustain you in the times of struggle. Learning how to effectively engage with your market right out of the gate will establish the precedent for the character of your business.

SURVIVAL KEY #8

Be Prepared for Challenges

When learning how to paddle a river, one of the most important elements to master is reading the water. Perhaps you've heard of an *eddy*. An eddy forms in a river when water passes by an obstacle such as a large boulder or a bend in the river. The water then moves in a circular direction creating a reverse current against the natural current of the river. I've listened to firsthand accounts of kayakers getting trapped in an eddy for several minutes, even up to an hour. Sometimes eddies are easy to spot. Other times they can be well hidden, and by the time you see one, it's too late and you're stuck. As a seasoned paddler, you learn to identify the signs of eddies and memorize their location on a river; but even then, water levels change, river banks erode, and objects alter their location. Even if you paddle the same river on a regular basis, you may not always know where you might encounter the next challenge.

There are "eddies," or challenges, that can appear in business as well. And just like a river, the key is knowing how to spot them early enough and what to do when you do encounter one. There are techniques for paddling out of an eddy, and there are ways to deal with getting unstuck from the challenges of business as well. First and foremost, however, you must develop the proper attitude for dealing with those challenges. You can't panic on the river, and you can't panic in business. As the saying goes: 10% of life is what happens to you, 90% is how you react to it.

You're probably familiar with the A/B personality theory. Type A personalities tend to be more driven and organized. They like to plan and like it when things go as planned. Type B personalities tend to be more creative and reflective. Like so many entrepreneurs, I fall into the Type B category. But as a business owner I have had to develop the A side of my personality, because drive and organization are essential traits in business ownership.

Those of us who are Type B personalities tend to treat situations with less urgency than we probably should. We have an "I'll figure it out later" attitude. Those of us with that natural bent need to develop disciplines that override those tendencies and keep things in check. At the same time, the things we can't control don't really scare us that much. Type B's embrace last-minute opportunities, changes, and challenges, which is why I think so many entrepreneurs tend to fall into that category. We naturally love shifting direction mid-stream to embrace something new. On the other hand, Type A personalities love to plan ahead and be fully prepared before moving ahead with anything. Each one of these personality traits can be an asset or a liability in business.

Ultimately, much of what leads to a successful business instead of failed one is how the business owner(s) and their team respond to the things they can't control or predict. If you fall under that Type A category, you may need to learn how to cope in situations where things don't go exactly as you planned, and how to stay cool under pressure. If you're a Type B, you may need to learn to counteract your procrastination tendencies and become a more steady, reliable leader.

But beyond developing your personal attitude in dealing with challenges, one of the keys to overcoming challenges in business is to know where those challenges originate. It all comes back to being prepared. While I can't tell you specifically what that means for your business, the first step is to identify if the source of the challenge is from an internal source—in other words the challenge was self-induced—or if it was caused by an external source.

Internal Challenges

Internal challenges can be identified as a problem in one of two areas: people or process. Immature business owners tend to be quick to point the finger at employees, partners, or customers when something goes wrong. Sometimes that's exactly where the finger needs to be pointed. However, if you've followed the steps outlined in this book I believe you can mitigate most of those potential personnel challenges in advance.

First, if you think your problem is people-related, revisit your org chart and job descriptions to see if your challenges are a result of something happening that contradicts that structure. Is someone not fulfilling his role? Perhaps, but more than likely, internal challenges are a result of a breakdown in process, not people. In fact, in my experience, when the challenge can be attributed to an individual, it's usually still related to some type of process breakdown that affected his motivation or ability to do his job.

When you first launch a business, you may be able to handle all the needs of your clients or customers by yourself. That obviously puts a ceiling on your potential. As you grow, you'll encounter not only an increase in clients to serve but a wider variety of client types and ever-evolving demands. The only way to handle that is with proper process. Every company, from the one-person consulting firm to the Fortune 500 company, lives and dies by its processes.

At Navigate, we went through a season during which we suffered some setbacks in spite of the company experiencing overall growth. Over a period of about a year we lost a few clients and fought through cashflow problems. Naturally, we looked for who was screwing up. We were building a fast-moving train, and everyone was on board. The culture was positive and the quality of work was as good as it had ever been. How could clients be frustrated and the bank account be dwindling? Our first assessment was that we had taken on some "bad" clients and we'd need to replace them with better ones to maintain our cashflow. But when we replaced them, we continued to experience similar problems.

While we certainly did take on some clients that weren't right for us, our situation begs a deeper question: why did we take them on in the first place? Was it their fault? No, it was because we didn't have the process in place to evaluate and onboard those clients correctly. We had good, hardworking people in the right roles on the organizational chart, but those roles weren't clearly supported by process. Deciding we had the wrong clients was an extremely narrow-sighted, self-preserving perspective. It was our process that was broken, not our clients, and we had to fix that before we brought anyone new into the mix.

Once we realized what we needed to do, we broke down the entire process of a how a client interacts with our company, beginning with the initial sales meeting and continuing all the way through the life of a project. We learned exactly how we were failing to set up the projects for success. Our clients didn't really understand how our process worked. They were excited about the potential results of working with us, but within two to three months they felt lost and confused. We were communicating with them, but they didn't understand that communication as it related to the overall goal of our relationship and the process we were internally using to accomplish their goals. The confusion lead to anxiety, and that anxiety became a cloud over every conversation. Many started slow-paying as a result of the frustration, which of course was the cause of our cashflow issues. Internally, our staff felt like they were working their butts off for clients who just didn't appreciate their efforts or advice.

All the talent in the world cannot overcome lack of process. In fixing the way we brought clients into our company, multiple challenges disappeared as well. Profits went back up and relationships with clients vastly improved. Your business, regardless of the size, will never outgrow the need for constant improvement to processes. I recently rode with a driver for a large ride-sharing service, and we had a chat about what he likes and dislikes about his job. His primary struggle was with a process involving toll roads. The failure of his employer's system forced him to be in contact with them on a daily basis, and they had no mechanism to effectively address his problem. He contemplated quitting because he was sick of wasting time every day trying to get someone to solve a process problem.

The simple lesson is this: no matter what size company you are, never stop improving.

Occasionally, however, even after reviewing your process you will have real problems with people that need to be addressed. An employee or partner may not be living up to expectations, breaking policy, or is simply ignoring the structures and processes you've put in place. When you encounter this and have to address this situation, remember these words: let the business make the business decisions.

> *let the business make the business decisions.*

I don't mean that to sound cold, and I would never advise anyone to put compassion and understanding aside. However, we often let those emotions get the best of us and make poor business decisions out of empathy for one person, which can end up hurting multiple people. You have to be clear and decisive with people when they are not living up to the expectations of their role. I've had multiple tough conversations with employees in my career and have had to end several relationships. It's never easy, but if I won't address the problems then I have no business being in business. You're hurting everyone by letting the problem sit. In business you need to become very good at letting personal emotion take a back seat to good decision making.

Now let's transition to the other side of the equation.

External Challenges

Around the year 2000, we started to experience a massive global shift in commerce. The Internet Age had reached critical mass and started to affect every business on planet earth, from the coffee bean farmers in Africa to the auto manufacturers in Michigan. I can't tell you how many times in the years following 2000 (even 10–15 years later) I heard people blame the demise of their sales revenues and profits on the Internet. If you're a golfer, you can blame the wind for every bad shot, but what good will that do you? At some point you have to deal with the reality of the challenge and compensate accordingly.

Every business was in the same situation when the Internet grabbed hold of society. Some instantly viewed it as an obstacle while others saw an opportunity. And some who at first considered it an obstacle changed their attitude and turned it into an opportunity. From retailers to stock traders, those who kept up won, and those who didn't have mostly vanished. You must face every challenge and first decide if you will view it as an obstacle or opportunity. If it's truly an obstacle, how will you fight through it and get better as a result? If it's an opportunity, how will you wisely take full advantage of it?

So let's dig deeper. First, we need to recognize the sources of external challenges just like we did for internal challenges. Most external challenges originate from one of two places: competition and government. These two external forces create a trickle-down effect in every area of business in every society on earth. From these two sources comes the unexpected, so understanding them will go a long way in helping you respond effectively.

Let's start with competition.

A friend of mine who owns a restaurant told me once that the best thing that ever happened to him was when a new restaurant opened on the same block as his. Sure, some of his customers now split their time and money between the two places, but having two places in close proximity also increased overall traffic to the area. The competition also forced him to improve his experience and product, which, in turn, increased the caliber of customer. And that resulted in both businesses making more money. Do the owners of both restaurants hang out together on the weekends smoking cigars in celebration of their mutual success? I doubt it. But they are both running more successful businesses because of each other. In his situation, competition was an opportunity to either race to the bottom by dropping prices, or raise the bar.

You will always have competition. Even if you're still in the idea stage, you probably already know who your main competitors are. They may be down the street or they may be online operating from China, but don't fall prey to the lie that you don't have any competition. There is always competition because there is always innovation. Brilliant young minds are sitting in college classrooms around the world thinking of ways to make the world better. The world is getting smaller and you need to constantly be aware of your surroundings. While you can't always know what competitive product is being developed or what attention-grabbing ad campaign is going to steal the attention of your customers, you can constantly stay ahead by asking yourself if you're doing the best you can to solve the problems of your customer.

Remember that direct competition is not your only competition. Thinking back to the outdoor equipment rental company I talked about in Survival Key #5, our competition for equipment rentals and camper rentals wasn't the retailers who were selling those items new. It was other businesses, like the cable company, that were com-

Survival Key #8

peting for our customers' time and money. We had to engage them in the narrative of an alternate way to invest that time and money.

While you need to be aware of competition, you must also be extremely careful not to obsess over it. Sadly, I've seen this result in the demise of several businesses. I have personally witnessed business owners become physically and mentally ill out of an obsession over their competition. Usually it's because they've seen someone who used to work for them leave and become their competitor. I imagine that's hard to experience, but all that does is confirm why that employee probably left: because the business owner was focused on the wrong things. You're not in business to beat the competition. You're in business to solve problems. If you do that well, competition will only ever be a secondary focus.

> *If your competition focuses on what you do right, and you focus on what they do wrong, they will win every time.*

So how can you turn competition into a positive thing? It's natural to criticize competition because it satisfies our egos. And while there may be areas where your competition should be criticized, chances are there is more you can learn from them than you can criticize them for. Your competitors probably do some things better than you. Pay attention to that. If your competition focuses on what you do right, and you focus on what they do wrong, they will win every time. Respect your competition, admire what they do, and use them as a catalyst to get better. If you choose, your competition can be one of your greatest assets. You don't have to like them, but you can respect them and appreciate how they force you to get better.

Now let's shift our focus to the second external force: government. Government is the most multi-layered, highly complex, and often dysfunctional entity ever created by humankind. When reading this section, please avoid the temptation to assume this is a political topic. I have no political agenda and my goal is not to influence you to one side or the other, but to simply provide a realistic picture of how government at every level will directly and indirectly affect you as a business owner. To help illustrate this point let's turn to an unlikely place: the comic strip *Calvin and Hobbes*.

If you've ever read the *Calvin and Hobbes* cartoons perhaps you're familiar with the game called Calvinball. In Calvinball, every time you play, the rules are different. And even within one round of Calvinball, the rules can change at any time. Each time you engage in the game it's different from previous times, and you never know what to expect. The overarching single rule of Calvinball is that it cannot be played the same way twice. Beyond that, literally anything goes. Look it up and enjoy a good laugh.

Honestly, when searching for the perfect metaphor for government involvement in business and economics, I am not sure a better one can be found. Tax laws, employment regulations, permits, and any number of variables will leave you scratching your head wondering who came up with this stuff and why. The rules constantly change, no one fully understands them, and most of the time they make your life as an entrepreneur more difficult.

Now, I suppose it is worth noting that not every law is pointless and without merit. But, it's the overall complexity of the thousands of laws and regulations and the constant changing (or threat of changing) that creates the frustration. Some of your direct interaction with government as it relates to business is actually very understandable and necessary. For example, you must register a business and pay taxes, and you can file for intellectual property protection when applicable. These are not bad things. They are there to protect you and provide infrastructure that benefits both businesses and society as a whole.

As a business owner, you have an elevated level of responsibility to your community to keep the role of government in check. If you plan to be profitable in business, you will be affected more than anyone else in society by every level of government. Small business is the lifeblood of every community, and business owners must pay closer attention than anyone else in keeping government working for the people and not the other way around. The failure of any society is when the government takes on the responsibilities of the free market and the businesses that function within it.

Governments also make a lot of mistakes. One small personal example: Our federal government literally created a company for me without me knowing. I started getting letters in the mail one day about a corporation with the exact same name as another company I owned but with a different federal ID number. There was no paperwork showing the company was set up. They just started sending letters about missing documentation. The burden of proof was on me to show that I did not establish this company or desire this company, and if I couldn't provide that proof, I was going to have to pay fines for the missing paperwork. Talk to any business owner, and he or she will probably have a story to share.

On a larger scale, the effects of government initiatives such as the Affordable Care Act in 2010 can throw businesses at every level into a whirlwind. Go back to the mental image of an eddy in a river pushing the current in the opposite direction—that's what it felt like in 2010. Small businesses had to completely overhaul their benefits packages, and large companies scaled their employee hours back to avoid fines and cost increases.

In 2016, there was a proposed federal minimum wage salary law that would have forced small businesses to increase the base salary of all full-time salaried employees to over $40,000 (over a 100% increase), or pay overtime. As an owner of a business that pays salaried employees, I was beyond concerned. The weeks when those employees would have worked over 40 hours would have cost us dearly, but we would have gained no benefit from the weeks when they worked less than 40 hours. It was legislation that could have crippled thousands of small businesses. Fortunately, that one was stopped by multiple lawsuits initiated by business owners who were paying attention and wrote their legislators.

Pay attention. Get involved.

Government is made up of people who are supposed to represent the best interests of their constituents. But all of those elected people have their own agendas and perspectives and can be heavily influenced by others. The perspectives and decisions of your elected officials will have a serious impact on your ability to succeed. Do yourself a favor right out of the gate and get to know your local representatives. Then, get a good business attorney and a good CPA. Nothing against your buddy who set up his own LLC online, but if you plan to be a professional business, hire professionals to work with you in handling your business affairs, or you will get lost in a sea of government bureaucracy. There are people who make their living keeping your business on track in the midst of the multiple tax laws and regulations. Focus on what you do well, and let them handle the other stuff. You have a responsibility to protect yourself and your business. You do that by utilizing the skills and experiences of professionals.

On a grander scale, there was a day when a business owner could run a small business in his or her town and not really care what was happening in the next town over—let alone in another state or on the other side of the world. In fact, it wasn't that long ago that other countries weren't even a part of the everyday business conversation. Today, however, we live in an era where what happens on the other side of the world affects every business in America. I have clients who are directly competing with companies in China, even (ironically) when selling to our own government.

We've all experienced it firsthand. The latest technology being developed in Japan affects the app developer in New York whose product is used on a phone built in China that was designed by a company in California. Then, there's a mom in the middle of Idaho who's using that app to find a local business to sell her a phone case that was made in Taiwan, while comparing that price to the price of a different e-commerce business based in Canada.

The global boundaries have been broken down, and the world's economy is your economy. These scenarios don't exist without governments. How the Chinese government interacts with the U.S. government can force you to change your business model, which again is why you need to pay attention. The trickle-down effects of both national and global economic policy will undoubtedly impact you directly or indirectly at some point, but that doesn't necessarily mean you need to be overwhelmed or afraid. Just like the competition across the street, a business in China or India can also be a huge asset.

If you're a manufacturer, for example, a foreign company may beat you on price for any number of reasons. Their cost of labor may be much lower than yours due to lack of government regulation in their country–meaning you could never beat them in a price war. You then need to find a way out of that price war and revise your model based on something other than price. You may have to revisit quality, financing options, service plans, or any number of variables to outsell them. In the end, these things strengthen your value proposition and may even increase your profit margins. You probably didn't start your business with a goal of being the cheapest in a field of commodities, so don't let someone else choose that destiny for you.

The American system of economics, otherwise known as the free enterprise system, was built on entrepreneurship. This system only survives when business owners have the freedom to take risks and pursue rewards with limited interference. The entrepreneurs are therefore the ones that can, and must, protect this system, or everyone suffers.

To bring this chapter to a close, let's go back to the river. I was paddling down the Colorado River with my friend, Sheri, who is also an experienced guide. As we approached the first set of rapids, she shouted at me, "Okay Rob, start paddling hard!" It almost seemed like a contradiction in that moment. As you start seeing the strange movements in the water, the eddies, your natural instinct is to think you should be cautious. But the key to paddling through an eddy or whitewater is to tackle it aggressively.

Sometimes when we approach challenges in business we want to be overly cautious. The reason for that may be because we lack confidence, especially when in uncharted waters. But, understanding how the challenge originated, combined with applying the other elements outlined in this book, makes you prepared to overcome anything that comes your way. Now go tackle those challenges aggressively!

SURVIVAL KEY #9

Always Be Brand Conscious

One of the most misunderstood concepts in business is branding. The word originates from the ancient practice of marking livestock to indicate the identity of the animal's owner. To this day, that same principle holds true in business. A mark (trademark) represents the identity of the business. Most of us think of a logo, company name, or tagline when we hear the term brand, but that's only a small part of the story.

In reality, your brand is the collective perception of everyone who knows you exist.

Think about the weight that statement carries. It means that your

> *Your brand is the collective perception of everyone who knows you exist.*

brand is ultimately in the hands of the marketplace. When you make that mental shift and start to think about your brand from the perspective of the consumer, you begin to realize how much energy it takes to build and maintain a great brand. It requires more than a well designed logo and clever tagline. A great brand requires being extremely cognizant of how the consumer perceives every aspect of your business—from your people, to your product, to your marketing. Your brand is how people feel about your company and how they talk about it. If your brand is not built right and managed effectively, all the hard work you've put in to developing your business could be for nothing.

Great brands are incredibly valuable. I once read that if the Coca-Cola company sold every physical asset they owned, the dollar amount would not equal the value of the brand by itself. I imagine the same could be true of other corporate giants such as Apple, McDonald's, and Nike. You could slap the Nike swoosh on a can of soup, charge 20% more, and probably outsell every other brand. Companies that have great brands–and as a result have great revenues–have those because they understand that the success of a business ultimately comes down to consumer experiences. I've said before that business is math, but branding is human. It's not about art or design (although those are important) it's about creating human connections.

Survival Key #9

Using Nike as an example again, I'd like you to think back to every one of their TV commercials you've ever seen. Can you recall a single ad that highlighted their products? Probably not. Nike is often put on a pedestal for their powerful advertisements because nearly every ad they've ever produced highlighted stories instead of products, and it's always worked. In many of their ads, the products are in the background (if they're even visible at all). The logo always makes a strong appearance, reminding you who's telling the story, but everything else, including their product, takes a back seat to the human experience that they're selling.

Take some time and search for Nike TV commercials online. Some feature famous athletes as the lead character and others feature children. But in actuality, to Nike, *you* are the lead character. You are moved and empowered because you can relate to the story. As a result, when you go to the store to buy new shoes, golf clubs, or apparel, you always look at Nike. Even if you don't always buy their products, they're always a contender for your business. Chances are you have something made by Nike in your home.

We already addressed the topic of storytelling in Survival Key #7, so I won't unpack it again, but I don't want you to miss the fact that storytelling is not just about how to create compelling marketing campaigns, it's about creating emotional connections. From there, elements such as a logo and tagline can serve their ultimate purpose. The Nike Swoosh and the tagline "Just do it" are there to remind you of the overarching story. Your job as a business owner is to constantly maintain a pulse on the stories you're telling to the marketplace, and the stories the marketplace is telling about your business. *That* is your brand. Over time, your logo and tagline will trigger an emotional response with your target audience based on how it reminds people of those stories. If you've built a great business, focused around your customer, that emotional response will be positive.

To take that a step further, let's think about how people actually connect with a brand. At Navigate, we developed a three-part approach to this that I like to call Triangulation Branding.

I remember traveling the country for my sales job back when GPS systems in rental cars were brand new, long before smartphones and navigation apps. I always paid the extra eight dollars to add one. GPS systems work because of a process called triangulation—by accurately measuring the distance from a single point to three different known locations, one can accurately locate the position of that original single point. Countless times, however, I found myself lost while the GPS could only connect to two satellites because the technology was still in its infancy. I would sit in the parking lot for several minutes staring at that little screen that said "searching for satellites." When the GPS system in the rental car lost contact with one of those three satellites, I became lost as a result.

When a business effectively connects to consumers, they embrace the brand as part of their own identity. Using Apple as an example again, this is why some people call themselves "Mac" people and not "PC" people, even though many times they can't explain why their computer is better. A great brand functions like a GPS system, connecting with your target consumers in three ways; visually, socially, and physically. Let's unpack these three elements of branding:

Visual

Visual branding manifests in anything your customers can see, beginning with the simplest items such as your logo and business cards. This is the one-way communication from you to your target customers. Visual branding has the greatest market reach because you can deploy it anywhere, from a local newspaper ad to a national TV commercial. Websites, brochures, and billboards are all a part of visual branding.

Your visual branding is often the first exposure someone has to your business. Today, more than ever, it's imperative that your visual branding looks professional. I can't stress enough the importance of hiring professionals to help you develop your visual branding and marketing assets, as I discussed in Survival Key #7. If you're not an artist, don't try to be one to save a few bucks. Just like you're competing against indirect competition for your customers' money, you're also competing against their marketing for your customers' attention. As consumers, we have standards that we've become accustomed to. We see hundreds of professional advertisements every day. If yours looks like something created on PowerPoint in 1998, you're already a sub-par company in the minds of your audience before they even know who you are or what you do.

Another part of visual branding is the words you create. Keep your writing simple. No one wants to read 1,000 words on your website landing page or in your brochure. In today's world, sitting through a 15-second commercial before a YouTube video is almost too much to bear. Get to the point, grab their interest, and let them dig deeper on their own through the pages on your website or by contacting your company. Visual branding is there to get attention, not sell. Keep it brand centric: Tell a story and avoid trying to highlight every little sub-narrative that you want to talk about.

Social

You've put time, energy, and money into great visual branding elements, your website looks great, you've got a professional video, and a brochure that's so beautiful it's hard to give away. Now you're ready for the second branding satellite: Social Branding. Social response can enhance or destroy the value of your visual branding in a matter of minutes. Social branding takes your story from the one-way conversation found in your visual branding to a two-way conversation between you and your potential customer, and between your customers themselves.

Until recently, social branding was very hard for a business to get a handle on. The most effective social branding has always been, and will always be, word of mouth. Nothing replaces the credibility that is carried between individuals who have a trusting relationship. Comments shared between friends can overpower any marketing campaign you initiate. Even if they're just Facebook friends.

As a business operating in our modern society, you have the ability more than ever before to direct the social branding that occurs in the marketplace. Social media has changed the game for businesses and marketers. The ability to post, share, review, and boost puts messages in front of targeted audiences at previously unimagined levels. It goes without saying that you should be exploring how to effectively utilize social media for your business.

To do so, however, you must first understand the fundamental rule of all social marketing: it must be conversational. Placing an ad on Facebook is not social marketing; it's just traditional advertising on a new platform. You and your employees should regularly be engaging in the conversations that are happening in your community and your industry. Position yourselves as interesting and credible voices in those conversations. Introduce topics and engage in activity on the various platforms that fit the nature of your business.

Always be cognizant of the fact that credibility is measured by association. Everything you and your team members say on social media represents your brand. Obviously, you never want a culture in which you police people's personal lives, but make sure your team members know that what they do and say has an impact on your credibility and ability to maintain a positive corporate brand, which ultimately affects your ability to create revenue. We've all seen news stories of an employee getting fired for something she said on social media. But on the other side of that, I have also seen customers leave companies because of the social media behavior of an employee. Like it or not, people develop

> *Credibility is measured by association.*

perceptions of you and your business based on your associations, and social media has the ability to reveal the character of those you associate with. Nothing you put in a brochure will override that.

Don't just be virtually social, though; be physically social. Sponsor causes, show up at community events, or initiate other efforts that fit the nature of your business. It's important for people to build a connection to your business beyond the virtual world. Branding is human, so have a human connection to your market. Customer referral programs and incentives for employees help foster social activity and that priceless word-of-mouth activity. Give your employees and customers stories to tell and reward them for doing so.

Physical

The third branding satellite is your Physical Brand. This is a concept that I've only fully embraced in recent years. I must admit that as a marketer, I had never really paid much attention to the continuity of a brand as it trickled into the physical space of a business. That physical space can include retail stores, offices, trade-show booths, product packaging, and even personnel. Sure, we all understand the importance of a great physical presence, but I often see a disconnect between it and the world of branding. The power of physical branding is why you see companies like

Apple spend so much on that box your phone or computer comes in. While it may seem like a waste of money, it furthers the attachment to the brand and fosters repeat business. You feel more confident about your purchase because of how you felt when you carried it home and unpacked it.

A few months prior to finishing this chapter, I visited a manufacturing company looking to launch a new employee recruitment initiative. When touring their facility, my team and I began by walking through a very stale and small lobby followed by some very stale and typical conference rooms—just as you'd expect in any large company. The rooms were nice and had expensive furniture, but they were extremely predictable. But once we were through the boring rooms, we walked into the main production facility, which was an entirely different world. Technology was everywhere: robotic arms, huge machines, comfortable work spaces, and impressive computers. The employees were happy and excited to be at work.

This company was struggling to compete for talent, and it's no wonder why! Potential hires would wait in a very boring lobby and then go to meetings in boring conference rooms. A potential hire was never being given a taste of what the company really was. They were surprised by our first recommendation: don't hire us, hire an interior designer! We could launch an amazing marketing campaign, but the moment people walked into the building they'd wonder if they were in the right place.

Perhaps you're a one-person business, so a retail space or office building isn't part of your immediate plan. Perhaps a trade-show booth is even beyond the physical space you'll ever need. Nonetheless, you have a physical brand—you. The most important part of a physical brand is the people associated with it.

Some people seem like they were born to be a brand. They are dynamic, engaging, and confident. Others are more introverted and being part of a brand is a very foreign concept. In either case, I encourage you to be authentic. Don't pretend to be someone you're not. Create a culture in which you and your people can be themselves within the context of a professional representation your brand. There is nothing more disengaging than feeling like someone is being fake. It fosters distrust, which is exactly the opposite of what you're trying to accomplish with a brand.

Never lose sight of the fact that the moment you become a business owner you also become a brand, especially if you're the face of the company. Branding is all about customer engagement, so you may have to sacrifice some personal preferences in the name of credibility in order for people to take you seriously and want to engage with you.

You are part of the physical brand of your company, don't let your ego keep people from connecting to that satellite.

If you think of your brand as the GPS system for your customers, you'll be able to develop strategies that help move them where they need to go and measure if it's actually working. If customers aren't engaging with your business, then either you're missing a satellite or something is wrong with one of the satellites. Always be brand conscious, constantly monitoring those three satellites, and your customers won't get lost.

SURVIVAL KEY #10

Broaden Your Perspective

I want to close this book by sharing one of the most profound things I've ever learned in my life: perspective is the most powerful force on earth. It is the difference between a terrible bike crash and an amazing cross-country journey, the difference between a catastrophic failure in business and an irreplaceable education. Your ability to put everything into context will not only help determine the success of your entrepreneurial ambitions, but your happiness as a human being.

> *Perspective is the most powerful force on earth.*

To give this concept some practical application, there are three perspectives that I recommend you keep at the forefront of your mind.

1. The "Why?" Perspective

"Why?" is the simple question you should be asking yourself on a regular basis when it comes to building a business. I've made it clear that profit is the only reason you start a business. But that's not the only reason you do something, it's just the reason you make that something a business. There has to be more.

Regardless of how confident a person is, we all need validation. That validation will ultimately come from knowing you're doing something that matters. If you studied Psychology in college, you probably learned about Maslow's Hierarchy of Needs. Abraham Maslow introduced a philosophy, illustrated by a pyramid, that scales our needs beginning with the most foundational: food and shelter, and peaking with what he termed "Self Actualization." I define that peak in a slightly different way, as: "the need to be needed."

In business, you need to find validation in something other than money and accolades. You need to feel needed. You need to know that what you're doing contributes to something greater than your own material gain. Before you go any further, make sure you have a very clear answer to the question: why? What is the pinnacle of the pyramid where you find self-actualization and feel that you're a necessary part of a greater purpose?

One word that has helped me frame the context of my greater purpose is the word *vocation*. Despite how many people use the word vocation, it doesn't just mean your job or occupation. Once again, my friend and mentor, Greg, steered me to this way of thinking. We're raised to think about our occupation at an early age. The question "what do you want to do (or be) when you grow up?" is based around "what job do you want to have?" And most of us would answer something like: teacher, doctor, fire fighter, etc. But that perspective is too utilitarian. Although occupation is an important part of life, life is about becoming, and being true to, the best version of yourself possible. Your vocation encompasses all areas of life: as a spouse, parent, community member, business owner, and whatever other variables are part of your time on this earth.

The word vocation originates from the same latin word as "voice," implying its role in your very identity. When asking yourself "why?' do it by asking if you're living based on occupation or vocation. Multiple people can have the same occupation, but no one else can have your vocation. There are two questions you can use to help define your vocation. The answers to these questions may evolve, but the questions themselves never lose their value:

First, if you knew you couldn't fail, what would you do? Does your current occupation align with that?

Second, fast forward to being 90 years old. If you could go back and spend more time doing three things, what would they be? If those things aren't a part of your life today, then you're not being true to your vocation. What matters most at the end of life is what should matter most today.

2. The Time Perspective

Related to the "why" perspective is the perspective of time. In fact, when considering your why, you can often define it by how you want to spend your time, or more importantly, how you feel you should spend your time.

Time is the only non-renewable asset you have. How you spend it, or invest it, is the most profound statement of what you value. I can think of no better way to illustrate this fact than to share this story:

An American businessman was at the pier of a small coastal Mexican village when a small boat with just one fisherman docked. Inside the small boat were several large yellowfin tuna. The businessman complimented the fisher-

man on the quality of his fish and asked how long it took to catch them. The fisherman replied that it only took a little while. The American then asked why didn't he stay out longer and catch more fish. The fisherman said he had enough to support his family's immediate needs.

The businessman then asked, "But what do you do with the rest of your time?"

The fisherman said, "I sleep late, fish a little, play with my children, take a siesta with my wife, Maria, stroll into the village each evening where I sip wine and play guitar with my amigos. I have a full and busy life, señor."

The American commented "I am a Wharton MBA and could help you. You should spend more time fishing, and with the proceeds, buy a bigger boat. With the proceeds from the bigger boat you could buy several boats. Eventually you would have a fleet of fishing boats. Instead of selling your catch to a middleman you would sell directly to the processor, eventually opening your own cannery. You would control the product, processing and distribution. You would need to leave this small coastal fishing village and move to Mexico City, then L.A., and eventually New York City, where you will run your expanding enterprise."

The fisherman asked, "But how long will this all take?"

To which the American replied, "Fifteen or 20 years."

"But what then?"

The American laughed and said, "That's the best part. When the time is right you would announce an IPO and sell your company stock to the public and become very rich. You would make millions."

"Millions? Then what?"

The American said, "Then you would retire. Move to a small coastal fishing village where you would sleep late, fish a little, play with your kids, take a siesta with your wife, stroll to the village in the evenings where you could sip wine and play your guitar with your friends."

That simple story had a profound impact on me when I first read it. In my heart of hearts I identified with the fisherman. But looking at my life and how I'd spent my time to that point, I had lived as the businessman. How great it is to discover these things in time to do something about it! If you're not spending your time doing the things you want to do and should do, then make a change. I'll go back to the introduction of this book and remind you of the number one thing I hoped you'd learn from reading it: life is too short to be lived as someone else.

3. The Relationship Perspective

I was recently asked what was the most valuable lesson I learned coming out of my failure in 2007. After pondering for a minute, I answered, "Relationships are the most important thing on earth. Ever."

When I think about every good thing in my life, they all come back to relationships. Every time. What is most important to me are my relationships with my family, friends, partners, employees, clients, and everything in between. When my relationships are healthy, my life is healthy. My relationships are what carried me through the toughest days. I have a wife who has never doubted me or tried to change me. I have a son who inspired me to get back up and become a better man. I have parents who supported me instead of saying, "I told you so." I have friends who didn't abandon me, and business colleagues who gave me a second chance. Without those relationships, I was without hope.

The beautiful thing about losing all of my material possessions is that I realized how little I actually lost. In the grand scheme of things, the perspective I gained about relationships was far more valuable than the possessions. The realization that I had so much to be grateful for was the pinnacle of success for me. When stress enters into my life, I go back to that perspective and remind myself of where true value lies. The relationships in my life are stronger than the chains of stress.

On the flip side, the greatest pains in our lives are the result of broken relationships. People who've passed, friendships lost, and business relationships broken. Those are the things that hurt more than the physical pain of a bike crash or the ego bruising of failure.

My advice to you is this: never forget that the value of a relationship is the relationship. It's too easy in business to look at everyone as a means to an end. We often go to networking events and social media sites to connect with people for our own gain, instead of connecting just to connect. Start seeing people for who they are, not as mere pieces to your great puzzle of success.

Why are we turned off by aggressive salespeople? Because they make us feel like we are targets for their gain. Don't make people feel like the only reason you associate with them is because you need something from them. Nothing drives me nuts more than having a great conversation with someone only to have it end with some sort of pitch. Actually, that's not true, nothing drives me nuts more than when I realize I just did that to someone else. Don't be that person, even on a small scale.

Survival Key #10

Yes, you need connections to make it in business. So if you need help with something, be honest and ask for it. If you develop real, authentic, relationships based around truly valuing each other, you have permission to ask for help. But if the only reason for the relationship is your own gain, don't be surprised if they see through that and the answer is always no. Develop great relationships for the sake of the relationship, and you'll be shocked at how easy the business connections will develop.

Those three perspectives will carry you a long way on your entrepreneurial journey. If you succumb to any of the dangers or risks in business—if you fail to survive in one area or another—perspective will carry you through.

This completes your survival training. But remember, survival isn't the goal. Survival training is just the first step before you embark on a journey. If you apply what you've learned in this book, I truly believe you will not only survive, but have an absolutely remarkable adventure in entrepreneurship.

Rob Stam, Author & Strategist

Rob is a 20+ year veteran of business ownership and consulting, and lover of all things outdoors. *The Entrepreneur's Survival Guide* is meant to be a catalyst to teaching entrepreneurs at all stages the fundamental skills needed to succeed in business.

Rob's journey has been one where the risks of entrepreneurship have cost him dearly, but also taught him countless invaluable lessons about business ownership. Those lessons paved the way for a restart in business in 2008, which lead to the creation of his company, Navigate. Through Navigate Rob and his team of professionals provide strategic planning and market-engagement services for companies around the United States.

Rob is an avid mountain biker, certified SCUBA instructor, and adventurer of all kinds. He resides in Michigan with his wife and son.

The best performers in every field, from athletics to business, have a coach.

If you don't have a coach, and would like some guidance in applying what you've read in *The Entrepreneur's Survival Guide*, visit **robstam.com** to learn more about becoming a part of Rob's coaching program.

For professional business development and marketing services: Visit Navigate at **navigateworks.com**.

Acknowledgments

As with any project of this nature, no one person can or should take all the credit. The list of thank-yous I could write is longer than the book itself, but to highlight a few…

Thank you:

To my wife, Chrisje, for putting up with me and not giving up on me for the past 20 years. I'm not sure I could write a better definition of love than to simply say: "watch how my wife does it."

To my son, Isaiah, for inspiring me to be a better man and to never lose sight of what's most important. I look forward to reading what you will write one day.

To my parents, for giving the middle-kid room to grow up, for bike trips, and for being much more good at english than me, and helping edit this book.

To Toddie (Sarah), for believing in me, taking a leap of faith with me, and being someone I can count on every single day as a friend and partner.

To Jeff, for seeing something in me when we were on opposite sides of a legal dispute, and then choosing to be in business with me 15 year later.

To Allison and Sheri for helping me regain perspective on who I am and what really matters, and for helping me rediscover my love of the outdoors.

To the entire team at Navigate, for working your butts off every day. For constantly striving to become better and do better for our clients. I am humbled (and proud) to lead people of your character and talent.

To Greg, for being a true friend and mentor through the good and bad. For not giving up on me even though you had every reason to.

To Seth, for countless hours of a listening ear and a voice of wisdom.

To Ryan, for always being a friend first and client second through ups and downs, twists and turns; and for being an positive example I can point to in nearly every scenario.

And last, but far from least: a special thank you to Alex, for not letting me give up on writing this book. For seeing something that I had lost sight of, and for working tirelessly at making this project into something we can both be proud of.

Made in the USA
Lexington, KY
07 April 2017